■SCHOLASTIC

Revisiting The Writing Workshop

Management, Assessment, and Mini-Lessons

Marybeth Alley & Barbara Orehovec

NEW YORK • TORONTO • LONDON • AUCKLAND • SYDNEY
MEXICO CITY • NEW DELHI • HONG KONG • BUENOS AIRES

Teaching *Resources*

FOR JASON—

Always behind me cleaning up my messes

FOR ANNABETH—

My new favorite little writer

FOR JOHN—

Always ready to help with his omnipresent red pen

• ACKNOWLEDGMENTS •

Our students,
the true risk-takers,
allowed us to try out new ideas
and switch gears mid-way when necessary.
We are grateful for their patience and persistence.

Cover design by Jorge J. Namerow
Cover photo by Comstock/Jupiter Images
Interior design by Kathy Massaro
Interior photos by Jason R. Alley
Interior illustration by Brian LaRossa

ISBN-13 978-0-439-92643-0
ISBN-10 0-439-92643-2

Contents

Introduction 6

Building the Foundation

(1) **Working Together in a Writing Community** 8

    The Basic Elements of Writing Workshop 10
        Mini-lesson 10
        Independent Writing and Conferring 11
        Sharing and Reflection 12
    Rationale and Support for a Writing Workshop 12

(2) **Creating a Space for Writing** 15

    Planning the Classroom Space 16
    Organizing Records and Writing Materials 18
    Scheduling the Workshop 19
    Creating a Space for Dialogue 20
        Teaching and Discussing "Story Sense" 20
        Effective Dialogue 22

(3) **Becoming Writers in the Classroom** 26

    Expectations for Writing Workshop 26
        On-task Behaviors 27
    Understanding the Components 31
    Finding Helpers 38

Creating and Sustaining Inquiry Units

(4) **Focusing Instruction Through Inquiry Units** 40

    Beginning Plans for the Long Term 42
    Writing a Strong Unit Plan 47
        Gathering Resources 47
        Planning for Supportive Questions 47
        Planning for Mini-lessons Within the Inquiry Unit 49
    Pulling It All Together for a Unit Plan 49
    Teaching and Talking the Units 52
        Introducing the Inquiry Approach to Writing 52
        Beginning an Inquiry Unit 52

Guiding the Inquiry 53
Maintaining Strength Throughout the Unit 54
Assessing Throughout the Unit 55
Helping Students Remember 55
Celebrating Success 56
Think Ahead, Think Backward 56

(5) **Planning and Structuring Mini-lessons** 57

Teacher-directed vs. Discussion-based Instruction 58
Planning Mini-lessons 58
Using Read-alouds in Mini-lessons 60
Modeled Writing 60
Using Student Writing in Mini-lessons 61
Thinking Through the Typical Writing Workshop Mini-lesson 63
A Recommended Planning Form 63
Strengthening the Mini-lesson 67
Student Responsibility During the Mini-lesson 67
Ending the Mini-lesson and Connecting It to Student Writing 67
Making a Transition to Independent Writing 68

(6) **Establishing the Workshop With Procedural Mini-lessons** 69

Creating the Comfort Zone 70
Twenty Days of Mini-lessons to Build a Strong Writing Workshop 72
Sample Procedural Mini-lesson 83
Portfolio Selection Procedures 83

(7) **Studying Audience** 85

Making "Audience" Accessible to Students 86
Generating Topics for an Audience 87
Teaching Writing Skills 88
A Predictable Plan for Teaching Writing Conventions and Rules 89
The Importance of Organization and Text Structure 91
The Role of Revision 94

(8) **Studying the Craft of Writing** 98

Looking Closely at the "How" of Writing 100
Authors as Mentors 104
Using Texts to Support Student Topics 106
Sample Author's Craft Mini-lessons 110
Using a Mentor Author to Enhance a Story 110
Noticing Craft Techniques in a Picture Book 111
Narrowing the Topic 115

(9) Studying Different Types of Writing 117

    Genre Experiences 118

    Making Genre Studies Meaningful 120

    Genre Studies 121

    Sample Genre Mini-lesson 124

        Writing a Memoir 124

Continuing the Conversation

(10) Assessment Within the Writing Workshop 129

    Opportunities for Observation and Assessment 130

    Anecdotal Records 131

    Observation Checklists 132

    Rubrics 133

    Student Self-assessments 137

    State-mandated Writing Assessments 139

    Writing to Prompts 139

    Determining Grades 140

(11) Writing Throughout the Day and Throughout the Year 141

    Writing Instruction Outside of the Workshop 142

    Sustaining Momentum Throughout the Year 143

    Celebrating Writing Accomplishments 145

    Communicating With Parents 146

A Reflection 148

Appendix 149

    Anchor Texts 149

        Word Choice 150

        Text Format and Structure 151

        Mood or Tone 152

        Passage of Time 153

    Professional Resources 154

    Recommended Children's Literature for Writing Workshop 154

Introduction

WE WENT INTO SCHOOL THAT MORNING TRULY WORRIED ABOUT THE DAY. It was going to be one of those days when, because of an assembly *and* the book fair, our predictable, comfortable schedule would be useless. We work very hard to maintain consistency, and we weren't terribly excited about pulling irritable students through an unpredictable day. But as any well-meaning teacher would, we had a plan. We thought about what we really needed to cover that day, and we adjusted the daily schedule accordingly. We knew, from experience, that our students needed to know the day's schedule up front, so as soon as we could, with all the forced excitement we could gather, we told them about the day. And then that's when it happened . . . the precise moment when we knew we needed to do serious reconsidering of our writing practices.

"What do you mean we're not having writing?" "Wait, no writing?" We heard raised voices, "aw man"s, and one clearly annoyed, "What?" It took us a minute to get our bearings. We had not for a second anticipated such a revolt. Half as a joke, and half because she didn't know what else to do, Marybeth got up from her seat and went to the classroom door. She poked her head out just to check that it in fact said, "Mrs. Alley's class."

On the way back to her seat, she said, "Would it really bother you if we skipped writing today?" The class talked for a while and for lots of reasons that made sense and a few that didn't make a whole lot of sense, it was decided— "Really, it would bother us if we didn't write today."

We started our conversations moments after school that day. There was proof, actual irrefutable proof, that what we had been trying so hard to do was truly working! Our students valued writing time! However, it didn't take us much longer to realize that we didn't know exactly what we had been doing. We would have been hard-pressed to explain to someone else how we had cultivated such an atmosphere. But at least we knew we were on the right path, and so we began to reflect on our process.

When we set out to establish Reading Workshops in our classrooms, we did so from the beginning. We had to make sweeping changes, redesigning our program from the ground up. We were getting good at helping teachers rethink and revise. But our work with writing was different. We've always had "Writing Workshop" in the classroom. We knew about the importance of choice. We were teaching writing mini-lessons in ways that made sense to us. We never really set out to establish a successful "Writing Workshop." In hindsight, we thought that by having a Writing Workshop, we were teaching writing.

But now, it was different. Now, we knew writing mattered. We knew that writing time was important to the kids. We knew they had a connection to this time. And, when we finally came to terms with this, we knew we were not doing enough in our Writing Workshops. We needed to make some changes. It was again time for us to rethink and revise for ourselves. We needed to redesign our writing program from the ground up.

We began by returning to those teachers whose work had, in the past, inspired us. We revisited Lucy Calkins, Nancie Atwell, Carol Avery, and Donald Graves. We also explored new avenues, the most important of which was the work of Katie Wood Ray. These leaders gave us new insight and renewed passion for the planning ahead of us. With each decision, we thought carefully about the needs of our students and the demands of constant assessment. In time, we began to see a new Writing Workshop emerge in the classroom.

We've learned the importance of treating our students as real writers with real things to say. We've learned the undeniable power of inviting the work of other writers into our classroom, letting these authors lead the instruction. We've learned that by taking a step back and really coaxing young writers to the forefront, they have a great deal to teach us about teaching writing. But perhaps most important, we've learned to do this in a real classroom, with real students, real challenges, and outside pressures.

In a way, this all happened because we gave up pretending we knew all the answers, worrying about our own writing insecurities, and some control. Our Writing Workshops are no longer places where students merely move through the steps of a writing process. Our Writing Workshops are now living places that invite our students to think, to create, and to communicate.

We know that through our renewed vision, we've been able to create a safe place for risk-takers and thinkers. We'd like to think that, within this space, students are pushed to find their own answers and their own voices. It is our hope that this book provides you with a way to reclaim a small part of your day—a set of plans to help you build your own successful writing community. Because really, it would bother us if you did not write today.

CHAPTER 1

Working Together
in a Writing Community

WRITING TIME IN OUR CLASSROOMS IS A VERY SPECIAL, VERY BUSY TIME. All students are hard at work thinking, creating, and making decisions. As we peek into a first-grade classroom, we see Victoria count out several sheets of paper and staple them together to make her next book. Joshua carefully chooses between markers and colored pencils for his book illustrations. Ella and Emily huddle together in a corner as Emily reads aloud the latest book she's written. Colton gathers a pile of books on snakes as he prepares to do research for his next book. And Diana pores over David Shannon's books as she crafts her own story. The classroom of young authors is alive, inviting, and hard at work.

We move into a fourth-grade classroom and see Morgan conferring with her teacher and revising her story. As we eavesdrop, we hear, "I want this part to sound like Cynthia Rylant. I wrote everything we had for Thanksgiving dinner and joined them all together with ands instead of commas. Listen: *Grandma had turkey and ham and sweet potatoes and mashed potatoes and cranberries and stuffing and pumpkin pie and sweet potato pie . . . .* I even used an ellipsis to show that there was even more." Across the room, Kenyon rewrites one of his older pieces, trying it from a new perspective with some humor. Ashlin leans over Savannah's desk as she shares her almost finished piece. The room is obviously alive with many varied activities. What is not so obvious, but perhaps more important, is that the students themselves are making their own decisions about their own special writing.

How have the students learned to be the ones responsible for the decision making in their writing? And how have they become aware of the techniques that authors use? How do they know how to incorporate these techniques into their own writing at their age? Young writers do not enter school with such big ideas about writing. All this success didn't come without a lot of trial and error on our part. Slowly but surely, we made the transition from giving students ideas for writing to teaching them how to write.

The Writing Workshop model provides our students time to write, choice of genres and topics, and opportunities to work collaboratively with others. When you think about it, this is exactly what we, as adults, need in our own writing lives—time, choice, and the influence of others. Why should it be any different for young children and their writing lives? In a nurturing and supportive environment, students feel comfortable to take risks. When time is valued in a classroom for students to write, students grow as writers. And in an atmosphere where children are immersed in literature, children look to authors to be their mentors.

It's not enough to provide direct instruction and modeled writing in our mini-lessons. We have found that we need to encourage meaningful dialogue about books. We want students to notice what authors do to craft their work. We want them to question the decisions authors make while writing a book. And we want them to try to apply some of these same techniques to their own writing. In this way, we feel that we can meet the needs of individuals while providing them with true authentic writing experiences.

Over the years, as a classroom teacher and a reading specialist, we have immersed our students in writing and have personalized Writing Workshop to fit the needs of diverse learners. We have met the challenges of working with early writers in first grade, we have witnessed the growth and progress of children in the middle grades, and we have celebrated the success of our fifth graders as they finish their elementary years and pass state writing tests.

Recognizing Author's Craft

Throughout this book we will refer to author's craft. This term is used to acknowledge all that an author does to put his or her writing together. If we think in terms of an artist's craft, we think of the oils, watercolors, acrylics, pencils, paper, photographs, metals, wood, and other materials that an artist uses in a unique way. Likewise, an author uses craft in constructing a piece. The author makes deliberate decisions as to the choice of words, the structure of sentences and paragraphs, and even the overall organization of the writing. The writer's craft also includes how the text looks on a page. To catch a reader's eye, the writer may choose to use large or small fonts, bold or italic text, wavy or colorful words, varied text formats, and attention-grabbing punctuation.

It is no accident that our students have rich literate lives. They are exposed to the writing of others—both professional authors and peer authors—on a daily basis. In all grades children are immersed in a variety of genres and participate in inquiry lessons on authors and illustrators. This exposure to different genres builds the foundation for their knowledge of text structure and literary elements. In addition, the inquiry approach allows them the opportunity to question the decisions authors and illustrators make and to find deeper understandings of how writing works. As they proceed through the elementary years, students continue to question the work of others and use this knowledge as they develop their own writing voice.

It is our hope that this book will show you why children view themselves as authors and how you might go about creating similar authors in your own classroom. To begin, let's take a look at the overall structure of Writing Workshop.

The Basic Elements of Writing Workshop

Here are the basic elements of Writing Workshop:

- mini-lesson

- independent writing and conferring

- sharing and reflection

Mini-lesson

Writing Workshop begins with a short, focused mini-lesson. We get the ideas for our mini-lessons from our students' writing, from our required curriculum, from our long-term planning goals, and from our own expectations for our writers. As we read students' writing and have conversations about their work, we determine what is needed next. It may be a lesson on author's craft; it might focus on elements of a specific genre; or it could deal with conventions of writing.

How the lesson is delivered may vary from day to day. During the mini-lesson, we might include a read-aloud, choosing to read from a picture book, a novel, or a nonfiction text. Mini-lesson time might include modeled writing. Or, we might also showcase some student writing to highlight success with a particular writing skill or strategy. The choice depends on the focus of the mini-lesson and the level of our students.

Whatever the topic, we know that our students need to see us as writers. Perhaps more importantly, we need to see ourselves as writers—not just teachers of writing. Our students see us as we consider a topic, as we revise an opening line, as we make decisions on word choice and as we recall the writing style of mentor authors when we need help with our writing. As students witness our writing experiences and realize what other writers do, they take on these same characteristics in their own writing lives. And, they get to see how we are also imperfect in our own writing. This is not a time when we simply hand down information.

Whether we are modeling writing, reading aloud, or focusing on a technique or writing convention, we encourage dialogue throughout these lessons. We want our students to explore text with us, tell us what they notice, and ask questions.

Independent Writing and Conferring

After the mini-lesson, students move to individual writing areas for independent writing. They gather their writing folders and materials and usually work alone. This is the time when students work independently, at various places in the writing process. During this time, students practice what they are learning in mini-lessons and in individual conferences. At this time students and teachers value relative quiet. (However, the extent to which we achieve this quiet has much to do with grade level.)

During this writing time, we move around the room assisting students with their writing. We spend this time conferring with individual students or meeting with small groups of writers. If we quickly glance around the room, we may see one student researching a topic. Another student may be looking through a collection of books by a particular author and studying the author's craft. Two students may be conferring and disagreeing on the ending to a written piece. Everyone is involved yet focused on different topics and in various stages of the writing process.

The time allocated for independent writing increases as the year progresses, especially with young writers. Typically, most teachers allow 30 to 40 minutes for this time. Students need enough time to sustain their writing.

This independent writing time enables you to assess the needs of individual students and the class as a whole. While conferring with a student, you determine what the writer is able to do and how you might help. These conferences also provide you with opportunities to see what your students need overall. Do they need a lesson on paragraphing or would that be more appropriate for a small group of writers? Are they ready for a lesson on writing a lead? Are their words "tired," and do they need more exact nouns and verbs? You will have a constant source of mini-lesson topics based on the needs of your students.

"Teacher to Teacher"

Not all stages of the writing process require pencil on paper. Students need time to think about new ideas, gather their thoughts, talk to others, and look through the work of mentor authors. When you look around the room, it's best to remember that "on task" does not always mean sitting quietly and writing.

Sharing and Reflection

Immediately following independent writing, we provide time for students to share their writing with others. During this time, students share finished work and work in progress. A student may need to share as he or she develops a topic. It may be too broad, and peers can help narrow or focus the topic. Another writer may seek help with a draft if he or she has not spent enough time developing the topic, and the writing appears to be just a list.

Writers need opportunities to share and celebrate a finished product. Yet, this share time helps not only the writer but all who share in the process. Although the author may have written a piece to entertain or inform others, those in the audience realize the role they played in the creation of the piece: assisting with the lead, helping find specific vocabulary, suggesting a setting, or even naming a character. The time spent sharing brings together the writing community.

In addition to sharing with others, writers also need to pause and look inward. As reading teachers, we know it is important for our students to stop and reflect on what they have read, not merely to close the book when they are finished. It is equally important, if not more so, to have writers reflect on what they have written.

Writers should reflect throughout the writing process—as they determine their topics and formats, as they develop their pieces, as they revise and edit their works, and as they finish and publish the pieces. Beginning writers may finish a piece in a day or two, but upper-grade writers may take days or weeks to complete a work. Since much time and effort goes into creating such a piece, thoughtful reflection should be a part of the writing process.

Rationale and Support for a Writing Workshop

Many leaders in the field of writing instruction support a workshop approach. Nancie Atwell first published *In the Middle* in 1987. In it she shared her experiences with Reading and Writing Workshops with middle school students. She believes that students need regular periods of time to write, that they should have a choice of what they write, and that they should have conversations with others about their writing. Thus, she structured her instruction accordingly and gave her students the time and flexibility they needed in a Writing Workshop. Although her work focused on middle school students, this same approach works for elementary students.

While we follow the structure of Atwell's Writing Workshop, we focus especially on the role and importance of conversation. We spend a lot of time talking about literary elements and techniques. We guide our students in questioning what writers do and the decisions that writers make. We feel this dialogue is critical as we study mentor authors and examine how an author's work assists us in our own writing.

In *The Art of Teaching Writing* (1994), Lucy Calkins recognizes the differences of student writing throughout the elementary grades while still providing them similar writing opportunities in a Writing Workshop. Like Atwell's middle school students, these young writers in crowded New York City public schools write about what they know and feel passionately about. These accomplished writers work together in classrooms rich in literature and peer support. Their time for sharing and reflection is highly valued as the children learn from one another, respect one another, and value the work of others in their writing community.

Carol Avery's book *And With a Light Touch* (2002) focuses on Reading and Writing Workshops in kindergarten and first-grade classrooms. She invites you into her classroom to witness the development of these young readers and writers. On the first day of school, her students write—even kindergarteners attempt their names. What a perfect initial assessment! Avery's work shows the close connection between reading and writing and the importance of authentic writing at this young age.

Katie Wood Ray has written several books on Writing Workshop. *Wondrous Words* (1999) focuses on the importance of immersing students in literature and studying the author's craft. By recognizing techniques that writers use, students value authors as mentors and apply similar techniques to their writing. Ray's most recent book, *About the Authors* (2004), focuses on writing with kindergarteners and first graders. Ray believes all students can write, and for those who tell her that they can't, she tells them, "Just pretend."

Young students learn the rhythm and repetition of writings, the organization of stories, and the lyrical language employed. With encouragement, this knowledge is then internalized and applied to their writing. As we work with young students, we recognize that the books they read are short, with simple text, and so we use those attributes as models for their own writing. Young children can then see the writing task as doable; all it entails is making up a book!

Ray's writings have strongly influenced our work with students. She believes that teachers need to teach students how writing is done and that this is best accomplished by having them learn to write from other writers. Ray states, "Rather than garnering ideas for *what* to write about from their reading, students are learning to take their own important topics and then look to texts to learn *how* to write well about those topics." Ray helped us realize that we needed to go beyond "writing about something" to helping students decide *how to write it*. It was her work that inspired us to take some risks in our own classrooms. Her work gave us the confidence to let go of old, tired writing lessons and activities. We began to follow the children's writing more closely, tweaking our workshop with each new day. We're awfully glad we did!

We knew we had been spending a lot of time sharing literature with students, and we knew our students were making connections from their reading to their writing. But this idea of specifically addressing the craft, of having students think of possible decisions writers make to construct text, was the missing link in our teaching and in our students' writings.

Using mentor authors and studying author's craft has made a considerable difference in how our students read and write. Throughout this book, we will share with you how we have tailored our Writing Workshop and its mini-lessons to incorporate literature more effectively and to assist our students in looking to mentor authors as they write. Classrooms that are rich in literature and that provide opportunities for real writing experiences lead to the best writing behaviors. Writing Workshop helps you structure your instruction and provides you the opportunity to create writing experiences that meet the needs of all students.

Further, we will show you how we build the foundation for the Workshop with meaningful conversations, how we plan our mini-lessons through inquiry units, and how we assist students in studying mentor authors to guide their writing. Because of these additions to our Writing Workshops, our instruction and our students' understanding are deeper and more complete than they had been in the past. This book is intended to help you move your students from *what* to write about to *how* to write and think as an author, all within the constructs of a realistic classroom, with the challenges and demands you face every day.

CHAPTER 2

Creating a Space for Writing

EFORE PENCIL EVER HITS PAPER IN YOUR WORKSHOP, IT'S ESSENTIAL THAT YOU CONSIDER HOW YOU WILL CULTIVATE AN EFFECTIVE WRITING ATMOSPHERE IN YOUR CLASSROOM. When we talk about a space for writing, we are certainly referring to your actual room. But we are also referring to the feel and tone of your Writing Workshop. There is something special about our daily writing time; it is somehow different from the rest of our day. These intangible, but utterly positive, qualities emerge over time as you and your students work together to cultivate this writing place. To begin this journey, it's important that you try to visualize the Workshop in your own room. Consider your students, your current room arrangement, and all other ideas you have to make implementing a successful Writing Workshop possible.

If you were to enter Marybeth's room, you would see busy first-graders everywhere. While Marybeth meets with one student about his story, the others are working independently: stapling pages together to make new books, illustrating books, talking with others about their work. When adults enter the room, they are immediately sought out by the students and brought into the writing community.

Anyone who works with young children knows what it takes to keep students on task while the adult is engaged elsewhere. The independence on the part of these young writers is quite amazing. Obviously this didn't happen overnight. The Workshop evolved over time as a result of Marybeth's establishing her expectations, visualizing what she wanted her Workshop to look like, and consistently being organized and prepared.

This chapter will provide you with the tools necessary to create the space for an effective Workshop. Organization is key to holding the Workshop together. By being well prepared, you will help students establish the independence they need to be self-sufficient thinkers and writers. This will then allow you time to meet with students in individual conferences or to provide some small-group instruction—all while the rest of the class is busy creating their own writing lives.

Planning the Classroom Space

You might now be starting to visualize what your Writing Workshop will look like in your own classroom. You see students actively engaged in their writing, partners paired up in corners talking about their work, and you conferring with students about their writing. It is an active, dynamic place where children are hard at work.

Let's think about your space where all of this great activity will occur. You want your Writing Workshop classroom to be organized and well run, yet flexible. And in order for that to happen, students need to know where they will work and where to find the resources and materials available to them. As you set up your workshop, consider the location of the following:

- **a meeting area**—for mini-lessons, read-alouds, modeled writing, and share time

- **writing areas**—student desks and tables; additional writing areas for students needing privacy or space to work with peers

- **conferring areas**—for students to meet with each other or for you to meet with students

- **material storage areas**—for organizing classroom writing materials

It doesn't matter if we work with first graders or fifth graders, we strongly believe in gathering our students around us in a meeting area. This is a place where we all come together to hear a read-aloud, to listen to a mini-lesson, to see modeled writing or to share our writing. Even if you have big fifth graders and limited space, try to find some way to have your students gather up close around you. This allows them to see the text format or illustrations in a book as you point them out. They can be involved as you relate a story that leads into modeled writing. And they can be near their peers as they share and celebrate the work of one another.

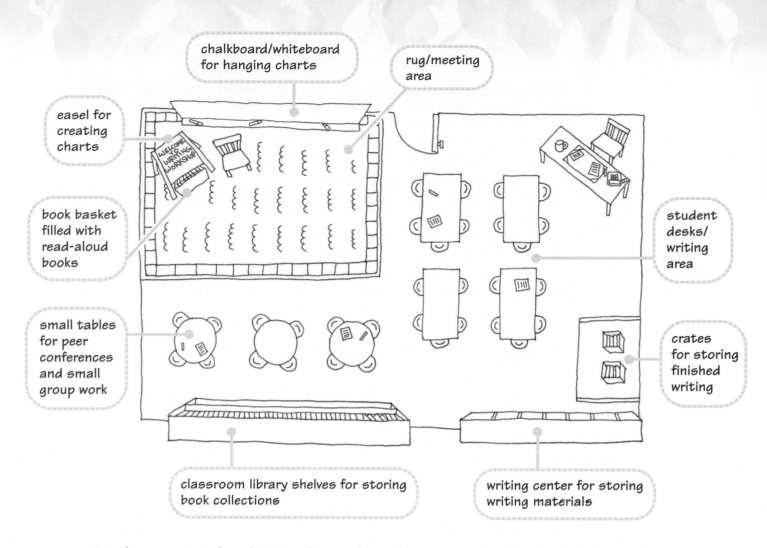

easel for creating charts

chalkboard/whiteboard for hanging charts

rug/meeting area

book basket filled with read-aloud books

student desks/ writing area

small tables for peer conferences and small group work

crates for storing finished writing

classroom library shelves for storing book collections

writing center for storing writing materials

▲ *Our classrooms provide a place to gather together and spaces to work independently and in small groups.*

The obvious writing spaces for students are their own desks or tables. You might also provide a special place or two where it would be quieter for students who need to work away from others. Also, take into consideration the needs of peer conferencing. If students are helping one another with their writing, will they be doing it right at their desks or tables, or do you want them to move away from others where it might be less distracting? And if they are to move, what happens when you have several pairs of students wanting to confer? Does your room have space for that?

Along these lines, you'll need to decide where you will confer with students. We tend to just pull up a chair next to a student to discuss progress and provide assistance. Although this is often done in what appears to be a random order as we "bounce" from one student to another, our records help us know who needs our help and who needs a follow-up conference. However, we know of teachers who prefer to have students sign up for a conference and to meet at a separate table in the classroom. These decisions are usually based on personal preference and the level of your students.

Teacher to Teacher

Our meeting area doesn't need a fancy chair, but we must have an easel with paper or access to an overhead projector. This is critical for our modeled writing. In order for the students to see us use the writing process, we need to save all of our work just as we ask our students to do.

Organizing Records and Writing Materials

As you consider your meeting area, students' writing areas, and where you will hold conferences, you also need to think about where you will house the writing supplies and resources. We recommend arranging materials so that students can help themselves to the materials as they need them. This contributes to the active atmosphere and frees you up for more important work—teaching. Such self-serve materials might include the following:

- hanging files for completed writing
- basket for recently finished work
- notebooks if students are to keep a "writer's notebook"
- clipboards for students who write away from their desks
- writing materials: various kinds of paper, sharpened pencils, erasers, editing pens, markers, colored pencils, crayons, staplers, staple remover, paper clips, scissors, tape, correction fluid, sticky notes, date stamp, cover-up tape
- word walls
- computers, printers
- picture dictionaries, dictionaries, thesauruses, electronic spellers
- writing resource books
- classroom library with book boxes for identified mentor authors
- charts of writing reminders or modeled writing

As you look over the list, you are probably asking yourself a number of questions. These questions take into consideration the age of your students, their previous experience with Writing Workshop, and the level of responsibility you want them to have. For example:

- Can my students get paper and supplies as they need them, use the stapler any time, and have access to tape as they cut and paste their work?
- Will students get their own writing folders when it is time for Writing Workshop, or will I pass them out as I send the students to their writing areas?
- Do I want to have some areas and supplies labeled *For Teacher Only* and *For Students* so students know what they can and cannot use?
- What do students need to do if they want to go to the media center for research or to use the computer? Will I have a sign-up sheet?
- How will I keep my records? What will I use for keeping anecdotal notes? Will I file away writing rubrics or other assessments?

Your Workshop will run smoothly if you spend enough time early in the year modeling how you want the Workshop to run. In grades 1 and 2, it's not uncommon for us to spend six weeks on procedural lessons. This time is shortened in the older grades, especially if students have worked in Writing Workshop before. You can show students how they can get paper and make books, how they can use a clipboard if they are sitting on the floor and doing some research, and how they can sign up to use the computer. You won't be able to anticipate everything when you first get started, and you might even change your mind about some things along the way. But by planning ahead and having a vision (even if it's initially fuzzy) of what you want your Workshop to look like, you are on your way to setting up an effective Workshop and giving your writers an inviting place in which to work.

Scheduling the Workshop

As you schedule your Writing Workshop, keep in mind the entire workshop time: mini-lesson, independent writing, conferring, and sharing. While the timing of each component is not always exact from day to day, the predictable ebb and flow of the Workshop routine is crucial to its success in your classroom. Student writers benefit from each part of the Workshop. We feel strongly that students are entitled to a lesson, time to practice their craft, and a time to share with others in their writing community each school day.

A Writing Workshop Schedule
Adapted for a First Grade Classroom
Approximately 45 minutes

12:50–1:05	Planned mini-lesson: read-aloud, teacher think-aloud, read-aloud discussion or modeled writing
*1:05–1:25	Independent writing time; teacher conferring with students or meeting with small groups
1:25–1:35	Whole-class share time; Workshop wrap-up

*This time can be stretched gradually to half an hour or more.

A Writing Workshop Schedule
Adapted for a Fourth Grade Classroom
Approximately 60 minutes

12:50–1:05	Planned mini-lesson: read-aloud, teacher think-aloud, read-aloud discussion or modeled writing
1:05–1:40	Independent writing time; peer conferences; teacher conferring with individual students or small groups
1:40–1:50	Whole-class share time; Workshop wrap-up

Most teachers would agree that time is at a premium in their classrooms. Often, writing time falls behind other "core" subjects. We often see teachers, on special schedule days, cut out the writing time. Finding 45 to 60 minutes a day seems almost impossible. We know we had to work very hard and a bit creatively to make it work in our schedules. But now we also know that our writing time is of great importance to our students. And, following their lead and insistence, we no longer simply just skip writing on days with difficult schedules.

Creating a Space for Dialogue

As you see your classroom evolving into a Workshop classroom, it's important to note how the discussions you have with your students both within and outside of your Writing Workshop works to shape the general atmosphere and students' writing. Throughout the day, whenever appropriate, but especially at reading time, we are aware of a few objectives that will certainly spill over into our writing space.

The following beliefs guide each of our lessons:

- Students who are aware of literature and how it works are more successful as writers.

- Students who realize there is much to learn from the authors we read each day are more apt to absorb the lessons of these authors.

- Students who can listen closely and follow conversations appropriately have more success learning from peer authors in the room.

- Students who can listen closely and follow conversations appropriately have more success helping other peers strengthen their writing.

- All of the above skills must be directly taught, refined, and expected by the classroom teacher.

Strong dialogue throughout the day goes a very long way in creating the writing space of your classroom.

Teaching and Discussing "Story Sense"

Story sense may not be a term you've used before, but it's certainly an idea that you've thought about. As you read and write with your students, you soon realize that some readers and writers just get it and others just can't quite make sense of it all. For whatever reason, many students lack a strong sense of story. Your job as writing teacher is to guide these students into the world of story where a beginning leads to a middle and a middle leads to an end, where characters work in relation to their setting, and where story theme flows naturally out of dilemma and resolution. This is the world of story—both in fiction and nonfiction—that first must make sense to the student *reader* before we can expect it from the student *writer*.

We teach story elements and text structure in order that our students may begin to make connections about what generally happens in good stories. Story sense allows students to predict, question, and self-monitor with ease as they become more and more independent readers and writers. Knowing how to look for and talk about certain story elements also prepares students to discuss and retell the story after they have read it.

Story Elements

Characters	▦ The people or animals onstage if the story were a play
	▦ *Can be flat (unchanging) or dynamic (changing)**
	▦ *Character studies should include a close look at how a character is developed through appearance, action, dialogue, and thought.*
Setting	▦ Includes location, time, weather, and so on
	▦ *Can be integral or backdrop*
	▦ *Setting can be differentiated from scene.*
Plot	▦ Sequence of events (beginning, middle, end; somebody wanted, but, so; first, next, then, last)
	▦ Problem and solution
Conflict	▦ *Man vs. nature*
	▦ *Man vs. man*
	▦ *Man vs. self*
Point of View	▦ Who tells the story
	▦ *First person "I" narration*
	▦ *Omniscient—all knowing*
	▦ *Limited omniscient—thoughts of one character*
Theme	▦ What the author wants us to think or to feel, the heart of the story
	▦ *Can be explicit or implicit*
	▦ The other story elements work together in order to sustain the theme.
Movement Through Time	▦ How much time passes in the story (a day, a year, decades . . .)
Change	▦ Something changes in each story on a large or small scale.

*Ideas in italics are more appropriate for older readers and writers.

The instructional emphasis of teaching story elements and structure is on helping students see that authors make careful and deliberate choices about how the story is presented. As you read out loud, help students to make connections between the setting and the problem or the characters and the theme. The more meaningful conversations you have with your students about story structure, the more interesting story structures will show up in your students' writing.

Effective Dialogue

One of our colleagues who teaches first grade often tells her young writers, "If you can think it, you can say it. If you can say it, you can write it." Not only is the language of this saying simple and easy to follow, it also gets at the heart of what we try to help our writers realize each day: Writing is an effective way to share thoughts, feelings, and interesting ideas with others.

Students who write well know how to honor words. They know that choosing words well takes practice. They also know that it's worth all the effort. These students have been taught how to listen for "words that work" and how to experiment until they find their own words that will make a piece "work." Teachers who teach writing well know that effective classroom dialogue sets the groundwork for these creative, risk-taking thinkers. Writing teachers must, therefore, strive to balance insightful showing and telling with active listening and questioning during each Writing Workshop.

As you might imagine, strong, effective talk among students happens because of the strong, effective, and carefully chosen talk of the teacher. There are a few key points that an effective class discussion leader must keep in mind while guiding students toward greater understanding of writing and of themselves as writers.

> *Work to strike a balance between "Let me show you what I notice," and "Can you share with me what you notice about . . . "*

We would not be doing our job if we never directly pointed out certain ideas to our students. However, unless we give over some of the discussion reins to the students, our young writers will never immerse themselves long enough to make any of the lessons or discussions meaningful. Their own writing will not reflect all the interesting "ways with words" you are pointing out unless students have the time to make it personal, to think about how a certain skill or strategy could relate to their own writing. We need to be sure we allow students to actively participate in the search for how writing works.

Teach, model, and practice conversation etiquette.

There are rules in place in our society for talking and listening carefully to what others have to say. We would not be able to hold group discussions in our classrooms if we did not directly and indirectly teach, model, and expect compliance with these rules. These routines and expectations are established early in the year, both within and outside of the context of Writing Workshop. Each classroom and each teacher will have a unique view of just how conversations should flow within a room. However, it's crucial to adopt and stick to a code of conduct for speaking in a classroom discussion.

Our talks will look like...

- All writers gathering together on the carpet
- Students raising hands
- Students putting hands down when someone's name has been called
- All students looking at the speaker
- Using the sign language "me too" to agree with someone
- Students thinking about what was just said
- Many different students talking during the discussion

Our talks will sound like...

- One person talking at a time
- Using kind words; we can disagree politely
- Speaker using a just-right voice so that all can hear him or her
- Using strong conversation words like, "I agree/disagree with (name) because... I can add on to what (name) just said... That makes me think about... I want to know more about what (name) just said"
- No repeating what another has already said

A classroom discussion "looks like/sounds like" T-chart completed as a class.

Teach (and expect) careful listening to others.

Especially in the younger grades, it is typical for children to know what they want to say, to raise their hand, and to not think about anything else while waiting to be called on. (And then, oftentimes, we are simply met with the admission, "Uh, I forgot!") Teachers who are skilled at drawing out effective conversation begin with small steps. They begin by helping young writers realize that part of the writing process is listening to others.

A first step involves introducing a rule that does not allow repeated ideas. A flat classroom conversation is one in which the same thought is repeated over and over (using just slightly different words) by different students. A dynamic conversation is one in which an interesting idea is shared and many students signal agreement, but no other student simply repeats the idea. Subsequent comments either add information that supports or negates the idea or look to another interesting idea to share.

Students can be taught to begin their comments with phrases such as: "I agree with Charlie because . . ." "I feel the same way, but I also think . . ." "I disagree with Alex because . . ." Depending on the age of the writer, this idea of piggybacking off other group members can be as simple as adding another example or as complicated as offering an alternative reason for something. The bottom line here is that with each additional comment, whether by a teacher or a student, the discussion should get deeper with reflection and closer inspection, not just wider with mere restatements and repetition.

Watch out for dominators and drifters.

Just as in group conversations with other adults, often one or two students emerge to dominate the conversation. These students, whether intentionally or not, tend to monopolize the discussion, often saying the same thing over and over again. And then there are the few students who seem to just drift in and out of the conversation, listening and then not listening, and every once in a while adding a random thought that is distracted at best. These students are clearly missing the opportunity to think deeply about the topic of conversation, and therefore they are missing the chance to see how the particular aspect of writing can fit into their personal writing life. Students can change their writing life after reflection, not after frenetic hand waving and disjointed attempts to be heard by others.

Pay careful attention to small, incomplete ideas and comments.

Often, students involved in a conversation want so badly to share that they offer only half of a thought. They might be unable to articulate their exact feeling, or, they just haven't thought their idea all the way through. It's important not to rush those whose thoughts emerge more slowly. It's also important not to try to quickly say in your own words what you think the young writer is saying. More often than we'd like to admit, we are not thinking the same way our students are thinking, and, their ideas are generally more interesting. Ask questions that might help you or other students see where the speaker's thoughts are: "What part of the writing made you think about your idea?" "Have we talked about your idea with other books or writings?" As adults who write, we know that sometimes all we have is a small, incomplete idea that will eventually turn into something more developed. We can help young writers to honor these small, kernel ideas in our class discussions. Just because a phrase is not polished, perfect, or even a complete thought does not mean it is without merit. When we take our time and carefully, methodically help our young talkers to think it through, we are helping them to see that ideas must grow. Big, wonderful ideas most often come from small, simple, nagging little ideas.

Honor all the voices, all the writers, in the room.

How class discussions evolve in the classroom has more to say about the climate and character of the room than about the writing ability in the room. Discussion about authors, their works, and their ways with words is part of the inquiry process in learning to be a good writer. Knowing how to act in a discussion, how to allow differing points of view, and how to move your own thoughts forward because of someone else's opinions goes far beyond the confines of the Writing Workshop. However, this climate of give and take is a necessary backdrop for the risk-taking that our young writers must do each time they thoughtfully put pencil to paper. These writers must feel they are in a safe place to say new things and write in new ways if their repertoire is ever to grow. We begin building the walls of our writers' safe house when we carefully and deliberately discuss literature and writing as a whole inquiring and encouraging class.

Creating a space to write entails much more than stocking the writing center. Successful writing spaces are filled with risk-takers, supportive peers, and plenty of opportunities to play with words and craft ideas seen in read-aloud books. It takes time to create this space. Every step is worth the attention, though. You are not merely teaching writing in Writing Workshop, you are creating a culture and a climate in which young writers emerge and grow.

CHAPTER 3

Becoming Writers
in the Classroom

ONCE YOU'VE DETERMINED THE BASIC FRAMEWORK OF THE WORKSHOP, YOU'RE READY TO START INVITING IN THE STUDENTS. The best place to start is with the ground rules of how you'll conduct the Writing Workshop. You'll need to think through your expectations for both the writing and the writers in your room.

Expectations for Writing Workshop

If you do not currently teach writing within a Writing Workshop, why are you considering the change? Is it being required of you? Do you feel that your students are not making the progress in writing you think they should? Do you feel you are not meeting the needs of all of your students? Did your students work in a Writing Workshop last year, and you'd like to continue that approach for them—or are parents expecting that it will continue? You need to be able to verbalize why you are making the change (to colleagues, administrators, and yourself). If you have not as yet done so, it's helpful to put a brief personal rationale in writing. As you do this, consider the following questions as you make the move to Writing Workshop:

- How are you currently teaching writing, and how do those practices mesh with the Workshop model?
- What areas of your classroom life would be most affected by the change?
- Do your students already have regular sustained amounts of time for writing?
- Is time allotted for your students to reflect and share their writing with others?
- Why do you feel learning to be a lifelong writer is a necessary skill for all students?
- How will the move to the Workshop model benefit your students?

By reflecting on these questions, you should be able to establish some goals as you generate a list of expectations. This is important as you organize your classroom to run a Writing Workshop. The goals you have translate into more specific expectations—expectations that are, perhaps, unique to your Workshop. For example, you may want your students to feel comfortable taking risks and sharing their writing with the entire writing community. If this is so, you need to establish a certain comfort level in the classroom. If you expect your students to write in a variety of genres, then you must provide the needed instruction and modeling. Take a look at the table on the next page that Barbara developed as she set expectations for working in a fourth-grade class. The expectations in the left column reflect her ideology while the right column indicates what needs to be in place in the classroom.

On-task Behaviors

As you consider your own personal expectations for the Workshop in your classroom, a concern you'll likely have is how to manage these independent writing behaviors. We have these same concerns whether we are working with first graders or fifth graders. In order for Writing Workshop to be successful, students must be able to be independent workers, to be responsible, and to remain on task. Even though it can be a very busy, active place, the Workshop must feel like a place in which writing can occur, and it must look and feel well managed—to students, to administrators, to visitors, and, of course, to you.

You may need to consider some sort of behavior management plan. This can be as simple or as detailed as you feel comfortable with and may include

Expectations for a Writing Workshop in My Classroom	Implications for My Classroom Environment
Students will know that they are a part of a writing community. We are not merely completing writing assignments; we are doing important work and sharing our writing lives.	An *ambience*—the room needs to feel like a comfortable place in which to write. Everyone in the room is involved in the writing process.
Students will write. Time is precious and so they will write about topics they care about.	*Time* to write and reflect. Instruction that assists students in choosing and developing topics.
All students will write. Students with special needs will meet with success.	*Accommodations* for writing will mirror those used to meet individual educational plans and goals.
Students will feel comfortable sharing writing from their personal lives.	A *safe environment* in which students feel comfortable with one another to take risks.
Students will have conversations about writing: their writing, the writing of peers, and that of professional writers.	An environment in which *dialogue* is encouraged in all reading and writing behaviors.
Students will use the writing process thoughtfully.	*Instruction*, *expectations*, and *assessment* of the process.
Students will record the titles of their finished pieces.	A *log sheet* to record titles and dates.
Students will be responsible for filing finished pieces and keeping all work in progress in appropriate folders.	A *finished basket*, *hanging files*, and *folders* for the ongoing work.
Students will write in a variety of genres. They will have experiences with and knowledge of varied genres.	*Instruction* on writing in varied genres. A *variety of books* will be available to use as writing models.
Students will recognize the successes of peers and share in their celebration.	*Opportunities* to work with peers and a *time for sharing*.
Students will be responsible for tidying the Workshop areas, caring for the materials and resources.	*Clear expectations* about where materials and resources are kept, and consequences when these are not met.
Students will attempt to solve their own writing problems before seeking help from others.	*Checklists* and *resources* for revising and editing.
Students will keep a writer's notebook containing notes, quotes, and ideas.	*Journals*; *models* of other student journals; *modeling* of how to start and keep a notebook.
Students will use mentor authors to assist them in working on their craft.	*Lessons* and *modeling* on using mentor authors.
Students will use resource materials as a reference.	*Dictionaries*, *thesauruses*, *electronic spellers*, *word walls*, and other appropriate resource materials.
Students will do research when writing—especially nonfiction material.	*Resources* available in the classroom; use of computers for *researching online*; time allocated to research in the *Media Center*.
Students will take part in evaluating their writing.	*Rubrics* developed in collaboration with students; assessment conferences for individual goal setting.

consequences and rewards. However, we feel an effective management plan goes beyond a simple discipline plan. The students need to feel invested in the writing community, to feel that they have a stake in what takes place so that they want to be a part of what is occurring during this time. This Workshop should allow all of the students to grow as writers.

Think about the following questions as you develop your own management plan to ensure that your students are engaged in writing behaviors:

- What must I do to ensure that my students know what is expected of them?
- Will I use the same rules for general classroom behavior, or will Writing Workshop require unique rules?
- Will I be the one to establish the rules for our Writing Workshop, or will students write the rules with me?

After looking over your expectations you may find that initially you want to be the one to establish the rules for Writing Workshop. You may feel that some rules are just nonnegotiable. We find that we already have a preconceived idea of the rules we want in our Workshop. In order to involve our students, we then ask them the appropriate leading questions. For example, if we want to make sure our students are listening to our mini-lessons to get the instruction they need, we ask a question such as, "Do you think it's important for you to listen carefully

Sample Writing Workshop Rules

1. I will listen carefully during the Writing Workshop mini-lesson.

   - I will not talk with my friends at this time.

   - I will raise my hand to answer or ask a question or share an idea.

2. During independent writing time, I will write quietly.

   - I will quietly work on my own writing.

   - I will confer quietly with other students if I want help on my writing or if they need help.

   - I will listen and think carefully when I have a conference with the teacher.

   - I will only talk about writing during Writing Workshop.

3. I will not disturb others who are writing.

4. I will be responsible for my jobs:

   - I will record finished pieces on my log sheet.

   - I will put finished pieces in the completed basket.

   - I will keep my current writing in my writing folder.

   - I will clean up at the end of Writing Workshop.

   - I will maintain my writer's notebook.

5. During share time, I will share my writing and will listen to and be respectful of the hard work of other writers.

You may want to have a few very simple rules if you are working with young children. We keep our young students on track by simply saying over and over, "Everything I do helps our writing to grow." With older students, you may find that, not long after you establish the rules, you need to amend them. For example, if students are not taking the responsibility for cleaning up, you need to bring this to their attention. At that point, they can help you write a rule to address this problem. Many classroom teachers have students keep a copy of agreed-upon rules in their writing folders. This way the teacher can discuss any problems with individuals and refer directly to this established code of conduct.

to the speaker when we have our mini-lesson?" If we want our students to buy into working in a quiet atmosphere, we ask, "Do you think you'll be able to do your best writing if the room is noisy?" The students will see our point and then help us write appropriate rules. See the sample rules listed on page 29 developed in a fourth-grade classroom.

After you have established the rules, whether with your students or by yourself, you need to consider how you will enforce these rules. Again, you want this to be more of a management plan than a disciplinary one. You want your students to *want* to be a part of the Workshop, to write with their peers, and to grow as writers. However, if you have a student not keeping one of the rules, then that needs to be brought to the individual's attention or to the attention of the writing community. If Joshua continually does not put his materials away, then Joshua's problem needs to be addressed. If Elizabeth is never willing to share, then you need to see why she is not feeling comfortable at that time. If Katie is just too loud, then usually students can help in letting Katie know that they need a more quiet room. These are the kinds of issues that typically come up that can be addressed either one-on-one with you, in a small group, or with the class as a whole. Consider the behavior and how students can help in the enforcement of the rules. Especially in the beginning of the year as we begin to set the tone, the share time portion of the Workshop more closely resembles a class meeting in which the class meets to discuss problems and possible solutions. Not only does this ritual help our writers to see that their input is valued, it also helps them to respect the place and the process of one another's writings.

Early in the year you can usually anticipate the kinds of problems that arise, such as those mentioned above. You can be proactive by planning ahead and addressing them before they become problems. Take a look at the following suggestions:

❋ Model, with another adult or student, appropriate independent writing behaviors.

- Getting materials
- Conferring on editing or revising with a peer
- Writing quietly
- Cleaning up
- Maintaining the writing folder

❋ Work one-on-one or in a small group with students whom you anticipate might have trouble with independent writing behaviors.

❋ Develop a plan for responding to unavoidable moments when something goes wrong. Use that day's share time to discuss what happened to prevent it from happening again.

Understanding the Components

Even with most of the management details taken care of, we still believe that much of the success we enjoy in our writing classes is due mainly to the sheer predictability of each Workshop. All writers know what to expect—a comfort that goes a long way toward classroom management. It's essential that both students and teachers understand what happens during each part of the Workshop. Knowledge of how the Workshop works is power for all participants.

As we've discussed, there are three basic components of the Writing Workshop:

- **mini-lesson**
- **independent writing and conferring**
- **sharing and reflection**

The mini-lesson sets the tone for the day's workshop. It calls the class together as a writing community, and it provides a valuable vehicle for direct instruction of writing skills. Although "mini-lesson" implies that it is a short lesson, some days it is a little on the longer side. This may be especially true in the beginning of the year because your lessons will focus on procedures and management. Mini-lessons may also be longer when you incorporate a read-aloud into the lesson. Looking ahead as you plan into the next week or so helps you to balance the different types of instruction for mini-lessons. In this way you are still able to meet the students' needs and give them an adequate amount of writing time. See Chapter 5 for more on planning for mini-lessons.

Students in a Writing Workshop need regular, sustained periods of time to write. In addition, the time allocated for independent writing needs to be sufficient based on the needs and the level of your students. Usually this portion of the Workshop takes from 30 to 40 minutes. A too-short period doesn't allow adequate time to become engaged in the process. Early in the year, students may only have the stamina to write for half the allotted time. With time, practice, and high expectations, most students feel that they could keep going even when the full time is over. During this time, the Writing Workshop teacher remains very busy holding individual conferences or meeting with small groups. Students use this time to fully engage in the writing process, using the support of strong instruction and thoughtful peers.

When the environment is set, students come to see this time as their time to play with, to practice, and to take risks with words and ideas. They know you'll be around soon to check up on their writing and to help move their writing to another level.

Steps for Successful Conferring

- Begin each conference with an invitation—"Tell me about your writing today . . ."

- Approach each conference with an open mind. Writers can surprise you and you should definitely let them!

- Listen intently to what the writer has to say. Look carefully at the writing he has to show.

- Praise what was done well or what was attempted. Be specific. Not, "Great Writing!" But, "I love the way you began by describing the setting. I feel like I am there."

- Think about what might improve the writing. Consider the writer's ability, goals, and writing in general. Choose one aspect that you know, with guidance, the writer will be able to incorporate into his writing. (The chart on page 34 may help.)

- Help the writer to see how this one aspect (perhaps correct capitalization or choosing more descriptive words) could enhance his writing, both in the current piece and in future work. Work with the writer on using it and ask the writer to restate the lesson (and how he will use it in future writing) back to you.

- Take good notes of what you noticed and discussed. Use these notes as a starting point in the next conference.

- Leave a reminder of the conference with the writer. For younger students, we often write reminders on a sticky note that is placed in their folder. Older children can learn to take their own notes on lessons learned and the decisions made at their writing conference.

- Ask if there is anything else the writer wants to tell you about. The writer should always have the opportunity to have the last word on his work.

- Be sure the writer knows exactly what he is to do when you leave him. This quick conversation ensures an easier transition between writing with one-on-one support and independent writing.

- Leave on a positive note. Writers need to see your help at conference time as a refueling, not a bump in the road.

Inviting Mentor Authors Into Our Conferences

As we try to bring the life of other authors into our classroom, we keep a small arsenal of "tips" from them ready at all times. Having a few powerful nuggets of information to use as we confer with individuals is helpful for those who need some nudging.

- For students who are stuck on finding a "great" topic, we remind them that Kevin Henkes got the idea for *Lilly and the Purple Plastic Purse* just from seeing a little girl in an airport. We invite the student to think about a mundane, true occurrence and try to embellish it just a bit to make it interesting.

- For students who need to do more research or think more carefully about their topic, we share with them how Robert McCloskey kept ducklings in his bathtub before ever writing *Make Way for Ducklings*. He knew he really needed to get to know them before he could write about them.

- To the student who doesn't really try to write about what's personally important to him, we remind him how much we love Eric Carle's books. These books always seem to be about small animals. He says that he remembers taking lots of walks with his dad while his dad showed him all sorts of little creatures. Eric Carle can make these topics successful because he cares about his memories of his father.

- Sometimes students do not want to accept help from peers or their teacher. We share with these students that Norman Bridwell wanted to name that big red dog Tiny. It was his wife's idea to name him Clifford. Sometimes, a different opinion does make our work stronger.

- When students need a reality check and a little boost to revise their piece, we mention how Mem Fox took two years and 49 drafts to complete *Koala Lou*.

We find lots of these little stories on book jackets and on author Web sites. Then, when one of our writers needs some advice, it's nice to offer the hand of "a real writer."

Possible Writing Problems and Solutions

Observable Behavior	Possible Teacher Intervention
A student is doing a great deal of sitting and wasting time. When questioned he says, "I have no idea what to write about."	▨ Refer student to chart, "Where do writers get ideas?" ▨ Recall together some of the books read aloud to discover where writers get ideas. ▨ Talk about important things in a writer's life: *What do you think/care/talk about a lot that you might be able to tell others about? How might you go about telling that information?* Always leave "stuck" writers with a written plan, so there's no excuse for "just sitting."
A student writes a whole book or long passage that has a very confusing story line.	▨ *I was interested in the part where . . . and then I got confused. I started to wonder about . . . but you never really told me about . . . Let's talk together about where your audience might get confused and how you can help clear things up. Remember we're always writing so our audience understands.*
A capable student is spending way too much time illustrating. Little effort has been put into the words.	▨ *There are some impressive illustrations here. I can tell your writing brain is hard at work because of all the details you've put into these pictures. But now, I'm confused about . . . and I think strong words would help to clear things up. You need to spend your time now writing the words to match these detailed illustrations.* Often with some children (who do not *need* to draw first) we make sure that they always write words first and draw second.
A story rambles on and on when it should have stopped pages or paragraphs ago.	▨ *I just loved how you told me about . . . and I thought it was great how you said . . . that part really felt like an ending to me. But, then you kept on going and I started to forget all about what you told me before. Sometimes writers need to be careful that they're not telling too much. Let's see if you aren't actually writing a couple of stories here.*
There is a great deal of redundancy in the writing.	▨ *Let's think about some of our favorite authors . . . When we read about Lilly, we learned all different things about her. In your writing, you tell me you had fun here . . . and here . . . and here. But I think your audience might get a little bored if you don't tell them something new.* Often we can get these writers "unstuck" by reminding them that writers often use repeating phrases effectively.
The writing is full of spelling errors.	▨ *Wow! What an interesting piece. But if you weren't here to read it to me, I would not have understood it. Your audience may be confused because many words are very hard to read. Reread your piece slowly and think about our word wall. You might also want to ask a good spelling friend to help out.*
Words have been omitted because the student worked too quickly.	▨ *It seems you got so caught up in your story that your brain was moving faster than your pencil. Don't worry. That happens to all writers. Now, read it slowly out loud and see if you can find some missing words.*
The writing lacks detail.	▨ *Can you tell me a little more about your idea?* Ask leading questions to get the writer talking, then leave the writer with a few key words that she mentioned to you. Offer suggestions about how to incorporate those ideas into the story.
A writer has made a good start, but gets stuck when it comes to moving the writing forward.	▨ Revisit favorite story patterns and books or authors that the writer might be inspired by. Think through possible endings with the writer.

As the time for independent writing draws to a close, you may find your students saying, "Oh, no. I'm not done yet," or "Just five more minutes, please." Use the last remaining minutes to help students make plans for tomorrow. With younger writers, we often write a few words or ideas down on a sticky note so they'll know how to begin the next day. You can also use these minutes to find writers willing to share a success. Whenever possible, select writers whose work or thoughts can help you finish the Writing Workshop by restating the main idea of the day's mini-lesson.

Immediately following the independent writing time, students reconvene for a short share time. This share time allows students to peek into the work of peer authors. It allows students to give and receive helpful advice and well-deserved praise. Share time also allows the writing teacher to again highlight the important techniques that she expects in student writing. The share time provides important closure for the Workshop and a way to help students see the connection between the mini-lessons and their own writing.

While we feel that share time is an important component of Writing Workshop, you need to consider how this time will best be used for your students. Not every student can share every day. Nor can every student share every finished piece. It not only takes too much time but, in all honesty, it gets boring. We want students to see the value of sharing with others and the time they come together as a writing community.

It's best if you know where you want share time to go before students even finish their independent writing. Take a look at the following possibilities:

- Choose a couple of students to share, based on how their writing on a particular day reflected your mini-lesson. "I saw some great work today while I was conferring with several of you. Karen will show how she changed the lead in her memoir after thinking about the book *Charlotte's Web*." This had been prearranged with Karen. "Billy also will share because he not only changed his lead, but he also changed his title." Again, students were asked ahead of time to share their hard work with their peers.

- Choose a student to share because you noticed something he took a chance with in his writing. Perhaps the attempt had been a result of working with a peer or using a mentor author to assist with his craft. "Before we close today, look at what David did with his story. He noticed how Jim LaMarche showed passage of time in the book *The Raft*. David tried something similar in his story to

The noise level in a first-grade classroom is not low. Children at this age are composing out loud, stretching words out to hear the sounds, and reading aloud what they have written. It is a time that you expect to "hear" the students writing.

✽

It's often best to give your students a warning when they have three to five minutes of independent writing time left. This gives them some time to wrap up their writing and to get ready for share time. Older writers can learn how to jot down a few notes on a sticky note or in their writer's notebook to help them remember what they are working on.

✽

Younger students often all really want to share their piece at the end of writing. To allow for this we hold a Share Circle once every week or so. In a Share Circle, the class forms a large circle. Students pair off with the one person seated next to them. One partner reads while the other listens and comments. Then, the partners switch roles. We bounce around, trying to hear as many conversations as we can.

It's important to remember that share time is not simply a show and tell time set up purely to entertain. Share time is yet another opportunity to teach strong writing skills. Students who share are carefully selected because their work has something to teach the other writers. We continually ask our students to listen to the writer and tell us, "What can we learn from this writer?" We end each sharing session by saying, "Thank you for teaching us that today."

show how the seasons changed. David, read the part in your story where you want the reader to know that time has passed and it is no longer winter."

❋ Allow a student the chance to share because he's tried something he's really proud of. It can be a time of celebration for a student who has been struggling with his writing. "Chris wants to show you how he used the book *The Little Artist* to help him with his own writing today. He noticed how the text format changed in the book and then tried something similar in his own story. Chris, talk about what you did with the text format of your book."

These examples remind students of the instruction that has taken place and how it applies to their own writing. It is also a short wrap-up for the day. Time is always at a premium in all of our classes, but once again, experience has taught us well—we should not cut corners and share time deserves its due.

Whatever way you choose to share with your writers, it's best though, for the teacher to have the last word, even in a Share Circle. We like to take just a minute to update the whole class on how certain writing projects are going. We do this both to keep the momentum and to keep making the point that writers can apply what they are learning to their own writing projects. "I was just thrilled to see how Veronica remembered to space her words today. She sure is thinking about writing for an audience!" "Jason's main character just sprang to life today when he added an interesting conversation into his story. He is remembering that there are many ways an author can show us what a character is like." In this way, the clear, concise language of the mini-lesson lingers with the writers, creating a natural flow into the next day's Writing Workshop.

Charley shared a book she wrote after reading *Letters From Rifka*. She fashioned her book as a series of letters to a friend about her camp experiences. Books that contain characters who write are great to use. See the suggested list that follows.

Hannah Harrow
Raleigh NC

Dear Sis,

From Hannah.

Sophie Harrow
Denver, CO
USA

Written by: Charley R.
(Hannah H.)

Dedicated
to
Hannah
from
camp

Dear Sophie, I'm driving to camp seafarer. It is a sailing camp. I am going there for a whole month! I am nervous but yet excited.

Love,
Hannah

Dear Sophie,
It is in north carolina. It is a 3 hour drive. Mom says that you are having a great time in Colorado. Hope so. Love, Hannah

Dear sophie, We are finally here! My cabin number is 23. My counselor Natalia she is really nice! and my bunk buddy's name is Charley she is nice, too.

Love you,

Hannah

Dear sophie,
It is lunch time! Their food is Pretty good!! Mom and Dad stayed for lunch. Then they had to go. I gave them a big hug. I'll miss them!   Love, Hannah

Dear Sophie, I am having a great time. I miss you a WHOLE lot. I will write you soon!

Hannah!

Charley   AUTHOR'S note

these books are alot of series and they are about Hannah's and sophie's journey at CO and NC. So keep reading for more adventures!

▲ When students such as Charley share their writing, others are inspired to try such techniques or are encouraged to show their own writing attempts.

Suggested Literature of Characters Who Write

T he following is a list of books featuring characters who write. As you talk to students about becoming writers, introduce them to some of these characters.

- The Amelia books—Marissa Moss
- Arthur Writes a Story—Marc Brown
- Click Clack Moo: Cows That Type— Doreen Cronin
- The Desert Scrapbook— Virginia Wright-Frierson
- Diary of a Spider—Doreen Cronin
- Diary of a Worm—Doreen Cronin
- Donovan's Word Jar—Mona Lisa DeGross (chapter book)
- Diary of a Wombat—Judy French
- Dear Mr. Blueberry—Simon James
- The Gardener—Sarah Stewart

- Hey World, Here I Am—Jean Little
- The Island Scrapbook— Virginia Wright-Frierson
- The Journey—Sarah Stewart
- Letters From Rifka—Karen Hesse (chapter book)
- One Quiet Morning—Helena Clare Pittman
- Nothing Ever Happens on 90th Street— Roni Schotter
- Stringbean's Trip to the Shining Sea— Vera B. Williams
- Three Days on a River in a Red Canoe— Vera B. Williams

Finding Helpers

While not entirely necessary, having parent and community volunteers during independent writing time is extremely helpful. As independent as we try to encourage our students to be, they still require a great deal of assistance when it comes to crafting their writing in just the right way. With the help of other adults in the room, you have time to stay a little longer with those students in true need. Volunteers are able to put out the little fires that flare up around you and help to maintain on-task behaviors and a quiet atmosphere.

For these helpers to actually work in the room, though, you need to do a bit of training. You need to explain to them what it is you want them to do, how much help to give the students, and what your expectations are for the students. We have noticed that taking half an hour early in the year to train all of our helpers makes a big difference to our Workshop. It doesn't take long, and our volunteers seem to really appreciate knowing exactly how they can be useful. After this training, or orientation, we also have folders available in the classroom for our volunteers. When they come into the room, they pick up the folder, which includes reminders about how to help and a list of individual student goals. The following form is part of the volunteer folder we use in first-grade classrooms. It can be easily adapted to other grades.

A Guide for Volunteers at Writing Time

Having a "Writer's Conference" with a young author:

- Pull up alongside a student and ask an open-ended "How's it going?"–type question.

- Listen for "a plan" for the whole piece. If there doesn't seem to be one, see if you can help create a "vision" for the whole story (beginning, middle, ending).

- Ask, "Is there anything special I can help you with today?"

- Comment specifically on what is positive (remembered spaces, neat handwriting, all the sounds of a word written down, interesting "author's craft," and so on).

- Push, just a bit, to the next level.

- Ask, "What can you do to make this page (or these words) even more interesting?"

- Ask, "Is there a book that you've read that might give you more ideas for how to write this story?"

- Ask, "How can you make this sound more like a book you've read before?"

- Before leaving the student, make sure he or she is clear on what is to be done next. Ask, "What's your plan?" or "What will you work on as soon as I leave you?"

Spelling tips:

1. Tell student to "Say it slowly and write all the sounds you hear."

2. Check to make sure the sounds are in the right order.

3. Refer those who are ready to the sound song sheet or the chunk charts in their writing folders.

4. Help students solve by analogy—"You know the word *come*, that will help you with *some*."

5. All sight words must be spelled correctly. Tell them to use the word wall if needed.

To achieve the goal of having your students become writers in the classroom, both students and teachers need support and predictability. Teachers can find support from their curriculums, professional readings, from the assistance of parent and other volunteers, and from students' progress. Students find support for their writing through the daily mini-lessons, the conferences with their teacher, the craft they see in books, and the other authors all around their room. A predictable schedule, clear expectations, and a modest amount of organization all help to set the groundwork for a truly successful Writing Workshop.

An example of a handy resource for classroom volunteers

CHAPTER 4

Focusing Instruction
Through Inquiry Units

IN MUCH THE SAME WAY THAT WE TEACH OUR STUDENTS THE PROCESS OF WRITING, WE MUST REMIND OURSELVES THAT THE TEACHING OF WRITING IS ITSELF A PROCESS. As we delve deeper into the world of writing with our students, we realize that while the finished products are often awesome feats, it is the road to these accomplishments that has given us the most insight, joy, and proud-teacher moments. This ever-changing teaching process begins with a plan—a long-term plan that acts as a general guide for where you will take your young writers in the year ahead.

Through our work both in Reading and Writing Workshops, we have come to respect the power of both a good plan and a solid understanding of how our teaching should be organized into longer chunks of investigation. These investigations focus our studies around the big ideas of writing. Often we see similar plans referred to as units of study. Because we believe in the power of discussion-driven inquiry lessons, we refer to our units as our inquiry units.

We believe that students benefit most from instruction that emphasizes depth, not simply coverage of mandated standards. For example, students need to fully understand why writers use punctuation, how it can enhance their writing, how it is used correctly, and how it can be manipulated to suit a writer's needs. Such an understanding does not come from a few teacher-directed lessons on using commas correctly and then completing a few practice exercises. True understanding comes from approaching the topic differently. Instead of telling students the rules of grammar, we present them with many models of examples and nonexamples. We ask leading questions:

- *What do you notice?*

- *Why might the author have done that?*

- *How does it help you as the reader?*

- *How might you use this in your writing?*

We find that it is only after students have closely investigated writing topics, only after they truly understand the mechanics and the craft, that these concepts begin to show up in their own writing—our ultimate goal in teaching writing.

In order to allow for this depth of understanding, we must carefully set up a tentative year-long plan. We must be aware of the concepts our students are required to know, and we must balance these skills with larger ideas that all writers must know. Our concept of this year-long plan has developed and changed over a few years. We've seen what has worked, what makes sense to teach together, and how we can organize the writing skills and strategies into meaningful, recursive units.

As we worked with our young writers and approached our teaching from the "What do you notice?" standpoint, we realized that we needed to have a firm grasp on what we wanted them to notice. Our inquiries, then, are not totally student-driven. We use guided inquiry; we know what we want our students to understand at the end of each unit and the end of the year. The paths we take to this end may change, but ultimately, and across the grade levels, we want our writers to know and apply these ideas:

- All authors must write about what they care about.

- All authors have a plan for their writing.

- All authors must think of their audience when writing.

- All authors craft their work. They make deliberate decisions as they structure their writing and carefully choose their words.

- All authors revise.

- All authors learn from other authors.

We find ourselves again and again returning to these big ideas, regardless of grade level. Certainly, these big ideas mean different things to different-age writers. But, in the end, if our writers leave our classrooms thinking about these concepts, we have built a truly solid foundation for their writing futures.

Beginning Plans for the Long Term

You'll know you are truly ready to dive in when you make the commitment to sit down for an hour and try to make sense of your calendar and your curriculum. Although each teacher will (and should) approach this planning differently, we have a couple of suggestions to help you through the long-term planning process.

1. Know your state and local standards thoroughly. You are required to make sure your students understand these concepts. Start here so you know the minimum level of instruction. Very often, though, these standards do not approach all the subtleties of learning to write well. We need to turn to other resources to bolster our writing instruction.

2. Take a look at other professional resources for writing instruction. There are many books, videos, and Web sites that can help broaden your horizons.

3. Make a list of all the topics, skills, strategies, and concepts you know you'll want your students to apply in their writing.

Possible Organizing Themes for Writing Inquiry Units

Organizing themes present a challenge to students. By introducing our units with a question, we invite students to work together to answer these questions in order to get at the big ideas of the writing process.

- How will we become writers in this classroom?
- How do writers get ideas?
- How do authors really use the writing process?
- How (what) can writers learn from other writers?
- How do authors write for their audience?
- How do authors write in the _____ genre?
- What is a story?
- How can I organize my thoughts into an interesting text structure?
- How do authors use revision to make their work better?
- What can we learn about writing from _____? (an author study)

4. Now, take a closer look at the list of possible organizing themes for your writing year (page 42). See if you can group all of the skills from your list of topics (Step 3) under five or six of these themes.

This list of organizing themes is meant only as a starting place for your own writing curriculum. There is no one right way to organize your requirements into these themes. In fact, it is very possible to place the same skill into different themes. In first grade, we learn a great deal about punctuation while we are investigating how we can write for an audience. A fourth-grade teacher might focus her punctuation study around the unit "What can we learn from other authors?" It is also possible to pay more attention to certain strategies by shifting the focus of the unit. One teacher might only want to introduce the use of writer's notebooks to her students while beginning the year in the unit "How will we become writers in this classroom?" Another teacher who has had experience with the notebooks may want to focus an entire inquiry unit on "How can using our writer's notebooks help us to become better writers?"

5. Think about a logical progression for the year. Begin to plot your thoughts on the blank unit template (page 44). Consider what you really want students to take away from the unit study and begin to think about your end goals for each unit.

The following unit plans (pages 45 and 46) are sample year-long plans for two different grade levels. While you will see many similarities with the big ideas, older writers inquire to much greater depths.

Once you have this road map in front of you, it's most important that you remember that oftentimes the best sights are seen on detours from the planned route. Especially in the beginning, when you're still feeling your way around this type of instruction, new ideas pop up and new avenues must be explored. Most of our "best stuff" has happened when we surrendered our perfectly typed master unit plan and followed the wonderings of our students. One caution though— be sure to continually revisit your required curriculum. You can't safely stray too far from those goals. Go where the kids lead you, but constantly remind them of the big idea and guiding question of the unit. This big idea (built around your required curriculum) is meant to help you take back the reins when an investigation goes astray.

"Teacher to Teacher"

We need to help our students remember all that they are learning. You will revisit many of the lessons you teach throughout the year. They may take a different format, be taught because of a need that arises, or linked in a different way to the unit of study. Your students may have worked with you early in the year to generate a list of alternate words for *said*. That lesson may need to be revisited as you see the need for students to apply that lesson to their tired writing. Or, while you may have presented examples of how writers show passage of time in a story, another lesson may be necessary if you notice that students need to move their stories along.

Writing Workshop Inquiry Units for _____

(Sept./Oct.)	(Nov.)	(Dec./Jan.)	(Feb.)	(March)	(April/May)
Topics addressed:	Topics addressed:	Topics addressed:	Topics addressed:	Topics addressed:	Topics addressed:

End Unit Assessment/Portfolio selection:

Ongoing throughout the year in writing conferences, small groups, and mini-lessons if needed:

Writing Workshop Inquiry Units for First Grade

✳ How will we become writers in this classroom?	How can we make our writing ready for an audience?	✳ What can we learn from other authors?	✳ How can we write more like . . . (author study)?	How can we use revision to help our writing?	What do we need to know to write strong nonfiction?
(SEPT./OCT.)	(NOV.)	(DEC./JAN.)	(FEB.)	(MARCH)	(APRIL/MAY)
Topics addressed: ▪ workshop procedures ▪ sharing ▪ writing with peers ▪ conferences ▪ how writers get ideas ▪ the writing process ▪ using authors as models ▪ different types of writing (the possibilities)	Topics addressed: ▪ writing conventions (spaces, capitals, end marks) ▪ word wall use ▪ rereading for sense ▪ author's purpose ▪ writing for and with peers	Topics addressed: ▪ using authors as mentors ▪ listening like a writer ▪ role of illustration ▪ craft studies ▪ story elements ▪ story structure	Topics addressed: ▪ story elements and structure ▪ planning before writing ▪ text format *Text structures (any month)*	Topics addressed: ▪ revision as adding on to clarify ▪ importance of rereading for sense ▪ word choice ▪ showing, not telling ▪ leads and endings ▪ main idea and supporting details	Topics addressed: ▪ features of nonfiction ▪ researching for writing ▪ role of illustration

End Unit Assessment/Portfolio selection:

Creative Response: What is Writing Workshop?	Students will select writing that clearly shows an understanding of writing for an audience. Students will tell how the piece shows this.	Students will keep an "I can do that!" list of writing ideas learned from other authors throughout study. Students will share their own writing that incorporates some of these tips.	Students will select writing that clearly shows an understanding of the selected work of the selected author.	Students will select writing that has developed over time through revision. Students will explain their thinking through the revision process.	Students will research a topic and write a nonfiction book using ideas learned from the study. Students will share their thinking about how the book is organized.

Ongoing throughout the year in writing conferences, small groups, and mini-lessons if needed:

▪ Appropriate spelling (approximated or conventional), appropriate spacing
▪ Complete sentences with end marks
▪ Sticking to topic
▪ Making sense to readers
▪ Descriptive words
▪ Including a beginning, middle, and end
▪ Reflection on one's own writing

Writing Workshop Inquiry Units for Fourth Grade

How will we become writers in this classroom? (SEPT./OCT.)	How can we make our writing ready for an audience? (OCT./NOV.)	What can we learn about writing from other authors? (DEC./JAN.)	What do we need to know about writing historical fiction? (FEB.)	How can we use revision to help our writing? (MARCH)	What do we need to know to write strong nonfiction? (APRIL/MAY)
Topics addressed: ■ workshop procedures ■ sharing ■ writing with peers ■ conferences ■ how writers get ideas ■ the writing process	Topics addressed: ■ understanding author's purpose ■ mechanics ■ writing conventions ■ text structure ■ planning for stories	Topics addressed: ■ craft studies ■ author study: Patricia Polacco ■ author study: Eve Bunting	Topics addressed: ■ story elements and structure ■ planning before writing ■ research skills ■ text structure ■ dialogue	Topics addressed: ■ revising to clarify ■ importance of rereading for sense ■ word choice ■ leads and endings ■ varied sentence structure	Topics addressed: ■ features of nonfiction ■ researching for writing ■ role of illustration

End Unit Assessment/Portfolio selection:

Creative Response: Students will write a newsletter that informs parents of the Writing Workshop rules and procedures.	Students will select writing that clearly shows an understanding of writing for an audience. Students will tell how the piece shows this.	Students will share their own writing that incorporates some of the writing ideas they received from the authors that were studied.	Students will complete a historical fiction work. They will tell how it is like other books of that genre.	Students will select writing that has developed over time through revision. Students will explain their thinking through the revision process.	Students will research a topic and write a nonfiction piece using ideas learned from the study. Students will share their thinking about how the book is organized.

Ongoing throughout the year in writing conferences, small groups, and mini-lessons if needed:

■ appropriate spelling
■ complete sentences
■ sticking to a topic
■ making sense to readers

■ descriptive words
■ mechanics and writing conventions, legible handwriting
■ reflection on one's own writing: What worked? What new thing did I try? What was difficult? What have I learned?

Writing a Strong Unit Plan

As you might imagine, you'll need to prepare much more than just a focusing question for your investigation. While the question itself is crucial, you'll also want to take the time to gather resources, frame strong, supportive questions, plan for particular mini-lessons and discussions, and think about what you'll want to see from your writers at the end of the investigation.

Gathering Resources

We find writing lesson resources everywhere and anywhere. Obviously, the most important resource is our library of well-written, well-crafted books. They are our first line of instruction. Additionally, we want students to know about the life of an author. We find many resources about authors themselves. We use videos about writers and their books. We keep a collection of successful student work that we can pull examples from. We keep an eye on the newspaper and magazines for writing that has been crafted well. We consider ourselves to be resources. In every unit, we do some modeled thinking and writing. These written pieces are invaluable resources. They show, rather than just tell, what we're after from our writers. In short, we're creative with what we have to use, and we're always on the lookout for a connection to our writing lessons. We also find that the more places we can pull from, the greater the chance that our students begin to see writing as an "everywhere" sort of endeavor, not simply a school subject.

Planning for Supportive Questions

We often hear teachers lament the fact that they can't teach writing well because they themselves "are not good at it." They don't quite understand how they might be able to help others become skilled in the craft of writing. Planning inquiry units around supportive questions is the perfect safety net. Within the framework of an inquiry unit, we learn side by side with our students. Our students do not perceive us as having all the right answers. Rather, we listen closely to what our mentor authors have to teach us about the craft of writing. We construct the answers to these big questions together.

When thinking about what kinds of questions we'll need to ask, we need to consider our audience and our curriculum. And yes, especially with our more inexperienced authors, the questions are often leading questions. We'll take a look at the big idea, the organizing theme of the unit, and we'll consider all the finer points about writing that we can connect to this theme. This is how we begin to break down the larger big idea into smaller pieces of information.

"Teacher
to
Teacher"

It's important to remember that not all writing skills need to be addressed or "placed" within one particular unit of study. Many writing concepts need to be continuously addressed throughout the year. It's best to list these concepts separately on the unit plan. You want to send the message that you haven't forgotten about these ideas; you just want to give them the year-long attention they deserve.

Sample Supportive Questions for Specific Units of Inquiry

Unit Topic/Organizing Theme	Possible Supportive Questions
How will we become writers in this classroom?	▦ What things will we need to be writers? How will we take care of these materials? ▦ How will we talk/listen to each other? ▦ What can we expect all writers to do? ▦ How will I learn about making my writing better?
How do writers get ideas?	▦ Where do you think the idea for (this book) came from? ▦ How can book jackets and Web sites help us discover where book ideas come from? ▦ How can we decide what topics are interesting to write about?
How do authors use the writing process?	▦ What do we mean by "writing process"? ▦ How does (this author) use the writing process? ▦ How does using the writing process make my writing stronger? ▦ Does using the writing process always make writing stronger?
How do writers write for an audience?	▦ What about this book makes it easy for us to understand it? ▦ What about this book makes it interesting? How might I do that in my writing? ▦ What can I do to make sure my audience easily understands my writing?
How do writers write in the _____ genre?	▦ How can we tell this book is written in the ____ genre? ▦ How are all ____ genre books alike/different? ▦ What do I need to remember when I write in the ____ genre? ▦ How does this compare to other genres?
How do authors use revision?	▦ What is revision? ▦ What do authors say about revision? ▦ How can revision help me as a writer? ▦ What can I do to revise my work? ▦ Why do authors revise?

Planning for Mini-lessons Within the Inquiry Unit

Planning for and delivering instruction within the mini-lesson is where teachers feel safe. It's in these mini-lesson plans that we feel we are "covering" required topics. For example, in the third-grade unit "How can I look again?" the teacher knows that he must, at a minimum, plan for and teach the following mini-lesson or series of mini-lessons:

- What does it mean to revise?
- How have we seen other authors show their revision?
- Writers revise to make sure their piece sounds correct.
- Writers look back over their work to check on mechanics.
- Writers look back over their work to be sure the writing makes sense.

Within each inquiry unit, there are basically two types of mini-lessons—those that you've planned on teaching all along and those that you find you need to teach as you work with your students throughout the unit. When planning the time line of each unit, you'll need to leave some room for these incidental lessons. The more your students see you tailoring the mini-lessons around their discussions, the more they'll buy into the idea that this Workshop is truly set up for them as writers. They will come to see that you are not just handing down assignments, you're helping your students improve as writers and thinkers.

Refer to Chapter 5 for more detailed information on how to structure specific mini-lessons.

Pulling It All Together for a Unit Plan

You've got your big ideas, the skills you need to address, and what sorts of questions might lead you there. The next step is to write down a plan that will keep you focused as you work through each 4- to 6-week unit.

The following sample unit plan comes from a second grade writing class. The "skills to be addressed" section lists writing skills taken from the required curriculum. The rest of the plan presents the way these topics will be discovered. Such a method emphasizes understanding, not coverage of skills.

Inquiry Unit Plan

Organizing theme: _____

_____

■ **Skills to be addressed:**

■ **Resources:** (Possibilities include read-alouds, mentor authors, anecdotes from or about authors, student samples.)

■ **Leading questions:** (What can you ask to get students talking about the topic?)

■ **Possible mini-lessons:** (This does not need to be a complete list, nor do the lessons listed necessarily last only one day.)

■ **End-of-unit assessment:**

Inquiry Unit Plan

Organizing theme: How can I get my writing ready for an audience?

Second Grade—Oct./Nov.

■ **Skills to be addressed:**

Rereading for sense, capitalization, and punctuation, using resources for spelling, reading in peer conferences, editing marks, beginning/middle/end, adding details

■ **Resources:** (Possibilities include read-alouds, mentor authors, anecdotes from or about authors, student samples.)

● *Tell Me a Story*, a book about Jonathan London—he refers to reading to others to see what it sounds like

● Collection of Donald Crews books—what does he do to make readers understand?

● Big books for punctuation inquiry

■ **Leading questions:** (What can you ask to get students talking about the topic?)

● What about this book makes it easy for us to understand it?

● What about this book makes it interesting? How might I do that in my writing?

● What can I do to make my audience easily understand my writing?

■ **Possible mini-lessons:** (This does not need to be a complete list, nor do the lessons listed necessarily last only one day.)

● What is my audience?

● Modeled writing—what rereading for sense looks like

● Modeled writing—how to fix errors

● Inquiry into use of punctuation

● Review of punctuation rules

● Finding words in a picture dictionary

● Modeled use of the word wall and other resources in the room

● Having a peer conference

● Guided inquiry lessons: What makes these books interesting?

● Guided inquiry lessons: What makes these books easy to understand?

● Sharing of student samples: successful writing that considers the needs of the audience

■ **End-of-unit assessment:**

Students will write and share at least one book that they have written with the audience in mind. They will share how they reread and changed things. The work in this book should prove knowledge of capitalization and punctuation rules.

Teaching and Talking the Units

As you might imagine, these well-structured and strong plans are only the beginning. What matters most in our writing instruction are the conversations we have about and around the texts we read and the expectations we have for our student writers.

Introducing the Inquiry Approach to Writing

For many of our students, this approach to writing, or any topic for that matter, is new to them. Students often take some time to warm up to the fact that you are genuinely interested in what they notice. Be patient in the beginning. Accept all attempts. In the beginning of the year, it's best to remember that your main goal is creating the appropriate atmosphere, not securing perfectly sensible answers. More astute answers will come later if a writing environment has been carefully cultivated.

Once our students are well established in the routines of the Writing Workshop, we begin to let them in on the instruction that will take place in the room.

Writers, writing time is a very special time in our room. I enjoy it, because I'm no longer the only teacher in here. How many books do you think we have in our classroom library? . . . Well then, that's how many writing teachers you'll have this year. We're going to spend our time this year trying to learn about writing from the people who know it best—writers! We'll learn how to look carefully at their writing and to listen closely to what they have to teach us about writing.

Beginning an Inquiry Unit

On the first days of a new inquiry, we spend some time addressing the organizing theme of the unit. We want to see what the students already know or what misconceptions they might have. This is a crucial step to consider when planning for future mini-lessons. This idea of "seeing where they are" is very much like the *K* in a K-W-L chart.

Listen in as Marybeth takes her first graders through the beginning of their unit on revision.

Writers, we have now taken a long look at how writers live their lives and where their inspiration comes from. I've been thinking about an idea that seemed to come up with all of the authors we investigated. Did you notice, as well, that all of the authors mentioned that they go back and rewrite? Did you notice how they all admitted that the words didn't just come out right the first time? I think there's a message in there for us. I think perhaps we need to do some investigating into this thing the authors called "revision." Let's see if we can find some answers to the question, "How can revision help our writing?"

Let's start our investigation where we always do; let's begin by looking at what knowledge we already have about revision.

Student responses were varied. Here is a sample of what the students had to say at the unit's beginning:

- Norman Bridwell rewrites his books six or seven times.
- Writers reread to make sure it makes sense.
- Writers use funny marks when they see a mistake they have to fix.
- We need to check for spelling.
- Marc Brown changed what Arthur looked like. That was revising his pictures.

Marybeth now knows that her students have some idea of what it means to revise. They've begun to touch on the idea that *revise* means to look again. She notices that many remarks are based on editing for grammar and spelling. This will not be the main focus during her revision lessons. In first grade, she simply wants students to know that they must look again. If they find mistakes along the way to correct, then that's even better!

Guiding the Inquiry

The first lessons of an inquiry unit are often very teacher-directed. Students need to have some background knowledge for what it is they are investigating. You can't truly wonder about something you don't even know exists. In the beginning of units, we find ourselves saying things like, "Do you notice here how . . . ?" "I am thinking here about how the author . . ." Do you notice this as well?"

"What do you notice?" is usually a few days out from the start of a new inquiry unit. We also know that it is during these beginning lessons that we are able to mold the language we want the students to use in our conversations. We do this by modeling the language ourselves and by restating what the students are saying.

Barbara is leading a third-grade inquiry lesson on text format. (The inquiry unit is "How can writers clearly get their message across to their audience?") She knows that she wants students to understand that authors can change the format or look of the text and that this change must match the meaning or make sense in the story. The class has just finished rereading *My Little Artist* by Donna Green.

Let's take another look at how different text formats are used in this book. I notice something different between these words and these words. (Barbara points to two different passages, one in regular typeface and the other in italics.) *What are you thinking about this?*

"Teacher to Teacher"

Often during the beginning lessons of a new inquiry, we teach one mini-lesson for the sole purpose of introducing important vocabulary. We can't expect students to talk about a new idea or new genre unless we help them choose the correct words. For example, after exploring poetry for a few days, we begin a chart titled "When we talk about poetry, we'll use strong words like . . ." We use examples and introduce stanza, line break, white space, rhythm, and rhyme scheme. This chart stays up throughout the unit and we refer to it constantly. Students are then expected to refer to the chart when contributing to class discussions.

STUDENT: Some words are straight and some words are slanty.

(Barbara restates this statement both to clarify that she's heard correctly and to plant the correct language into the conversation.)

I see you've noticed that the words on this page are regular, while the words on this page are in italics. Now let's think about why the author may have done this . . . What decision did she make while writing this?

STUDENT: I notice on one page the girl is speaking like she was a kid. Then it's like she's an adult on the next page.

(Again, Barbara restates and deepens this comment.)

I agree. It seems as if the author is better able to show us who is talking by changing the text format.

Whenever possible, we try to connect a new idea to a place where we've seen it before. Often, we have a connection in our head, but the students remember another place they've seen it. It is this working together, teacher and students, that helps to create the depth of understanding within the inquiry units.

(Barbara continues.)

Let's think for a minute . . . Have we ever seen the words on the page changing because different characters were speaking?

STUDENTS:

- When we read that big book about Rapunzel, there were different colors for different characters.
- I read a book of The Three Bears and Papa Bear's words were really big, Mama's words were regular, and the words got really small when Baby Bear was talking.

(Finally, Barbara restates these comments and comes up with a concise way of summing up the group's findings that the writers can carry back with them to their desks, and, hopefully, to their future writing.)

Ah, so we're noticing that one reason authors use different text formatting styles is to make it clear who is speaking in the story. Authors make deliberate decisions about when and how to use differing text formats.

Maintaining Strength Throughout the Unit

We build useful momentum in the units when we inch students toward discovering for themselves ways in which they can make their writing stronger. Throughout the unit, it's necessary to keep reminding students of the big idea. In most cases, our language is predictable, no matter what the topic. We find ourselves constantly using phrases and questions such as:

- Why do you think the author may have . . . ?

- What do you notice?

- How do you know . . . ? What is your proof?

- How is this like other books we have read?

- How is it different?

- What strikes you as interesting? Why?

- Why was it useful for the author to . . . ?

- How might this help your own writing?

- What decisions did you have to make as you wrote this?

- Don't you just love how the author decided to . . . ?

- What are you thinking?

- Tell me more . . .

And when they start talking, we listen carefully and we restate their ideas whenever we have to in order to help students see the connection to the unit's main idea.

Assessing Throughout the Unit

All throughout the unit, our eyes are on the end-of-unit assessment. While we want to be sure our students are practicing the skills necessary to be successful with the end-of-unit assessment, we also notice what needs to be addressed immediately. Is a small group of second graders ready for a grammar lesson on commas in a series (regardless of what unit we are "in")? We'll pull them aside during independent writing time. If fourth graders are having difficulty adding dialogues, then we rework the next mini-lessons to address this. Strong units are built around constant assessment of both student work and teaching practices.

Helping Students Remember

A great deal of information gets tossed around during all these workshops. It's important that students have a way of coping with all this knowledge. In the younger grades, our charts are invaluable. Students know where to find answers and how to use the charts to remember past conversations. When we specifically teach a skill during a writing conference, we make a note of this skill in their writing folder so that they'll have a reference for when we're not right there. In the upper grades, many students have a notebook or a way to keep notes about mini-lessons and conferences all together. Even still, charts are a must in the upper grades as well.

Celebrating Success

Success breeds success, and the best way to get students writing in a certain way or with certain skills is to prove that kids like them can write this way. We do this by watching carefully during independent writing. Whenever we see a writer who has written something or decided something that shows a clear connection to the unit's big idea, we march that writer right into our share time. We celebrate together, talk about why the writing works, and push the other writers just a little bit more: "See, we've seen how (the mentor author) can do this, and we've seen how (the student writer) can do this. Now I'd love to see how you can incorporate this into your writing. I'd love to see you share your big success tomorrow."

Think Ahead, Think Backward

Somewhere about halfway through your unit, you're going to want to begin work on your next unit. With any luck, you still like your year plan and you're basically on schedule. You'll need to be ready to roll with this next unit when the current one is finished. Remember, though, the very beginning lessons of a new unit are not difficult to plan for. The fact that you start out each unit with a day or two of talking about what students already know gives you a little breather and lessens the new unit planning crunch.

Sometime soon after you've finished teaching an inquiry unit, you need to sit down and take stock. What worked? What went wrong? What connections did the kids make that will help you introduce the lesson next year? Write down what books you've found along the way, and keep track of any skills or strategies that you feel you need to address further. Add them to the bottom of the year plan so you won't forget about them, and then go back and take a look at the curriculum standards you're required to teach. You'll be amazed at how much you covered and the depth at which you covered it.

CHAPTER 5

Planning and Structuring Mini-lessons

 ANYONE CAN BE A WRITER, SOMEONE WHO WRITES THINGS DOWN. But can anyone be a good writer—or at least a better writer? We have found that the majority of our students enjoy writing. But it is through mini-lessons that we are able to provide students with the opportunity to make their writing the best it can be. We present mini-lessons in a number of ways—in read-alouds, through discussions of an author's craft, by modeling the writing process, and even by sharing conventions of good writing.

Effective mini-lessons don't just happen. You make them happen through your efforts and planning. You consider the needs of your students, determine where they are in the writing process, and incorporate the local and state curricula appropriate to your level of students. This chapter will help you with both the planning and the structuring of effective mini-lessons.

Teacher-directed vs. Discussion-based Instruction

In Writing Workshop, the mini-lesson is typically very teacher directed. This is the time when we provide necessary instruction about the writing process. We plan out the lesson and do the majority of the talking and demonstrating. Our students need our expertise on writing. They need to know what we know about good writing, about what writers do to construct text. They need to see us write, to see how to get those ideas on paper. They also need to learn the conventions of writing, to see how to apply that knowledge to revise and edit their work. Further, they need to see us look to other authors and writing experts for answers that we don't have and could learn more about.

During this instruction, however, there is a continuous, necessary dialogue with students. Through this discussion, we can assess their understanding and determine what instruction is still essential for their writing. Our plans may be modified on the spot. We may go back and think aloud about why we made the decision to write the way we did. If we realize that the majority of students wasn't ready for a particular lesson but a small group of students was hungry for it, we meet with that group separately. By continuing to model and demonstrate good writing behaviors and letting the students in on the thinking we do as we write, we invite them into the process that good writers use as they construct text. We clarify what can be a very transparent process. By encouraging their thoughts and questions in an open dialogue, we further invite them into learning and sharing with one another. Our goal is not to *tell* students how to write but to *show* them how it's done. We show them through our own writing, through the work of published authors, and through their peers' writing.

Planning Mini-lessons

For planning purposes, we recognize three different types of mini-lessons:

- Procedures and management
- Writing process (including skills and conventions)
- Author's craft and techniques

These distinctions do not need to be made with the students. While this book covers each type of mini-lesson and suggests possible topics, we focus on how sharing literature and discussing author's craft can make a noticeable difference in your students' writing.

When we plan mini-lessons, we consider the needs and levels of our students. We know that in a typical classroom, students vary greatly. Similarly, in a true Writing Workshop, students are working at various stages in the writing process and are writing in various genres. While one student may just be starting a new piece, several others may be finishing up their work, and the majority is somewhere between drafting and/or revising and editing. So, we often find ourselves wondering, "What do I teach? What do my students need?"

Whatever we teach in Writing Workshop provides students with instruction they need. They may not need it on that particular day, but it will be needed. That is why we often find it important to record our lessons in some fashion on charts. Each lesson may not need its own chart; it may be information that can be added to previously developed charts. For example, one chart may be a work in progress on various forms of story structure. Another chart may have suggestions for writing leads for a story. In this way, students can refer to the charts as they need them.

There are also times that we have a topic planned for a mini-lesson and, as we set the stage and make the connection, we realize that students have questions and seem confused. We pay attention to those signals, go back and revisit the previous topic where there seems to be confusion, and save the planned mini-lesson for the next day. If they are not ready for the lesson, it will not stick with them.

Teaching writing effectively requires us to carefully consider how to best deliver instruction. Much of the strength of a mini-lesson comes from the close connection between lesson topic and method of instruction. When trying to polish students' use of descriptive nouns, it makes sense to include a read-aloud that effectively shows this word choice. It does not make sense to share the work of a student writer who is still learning the craft. When we wish to see more revision in students' writing, it makes sense to model the process and then to show successful examples of student writers.

Let's take a look at several ways to structure mini-lessons so they are successful.

Using Read-alouds in Mini-lessons

Our students participate in both Reading and Writing Workshops. As a result, they are exposed to a rich variety of literature. In Reading Workshop, we use read-alouds to teach lessons that support strategic reading. As we read these books, we model these reading strategies. Students see us stopping and thinking aloud and asking questions as we read. This parallels what they see us doing as we write in our Writing Workshop mini-lessons.

Our children know books, and so they ask questions and develop theories of what authors do to create books. "Why did the author create the main character as a boy when we know the book is based on her life?" "Why did the author illustrate this book when she hadn't illustrated other books?" "Why did the author provide a surprise ending to the story?" "Why is there only one sentence on this page?" "How did the author come up with such good similes?" Initially, these questions don't just pop out of our students' minds. Through our work with books and our modeled questions, we've led our students to think about writing decisions. In time, they are the ones asking the questions, and we are always amazed at the types of questions they are able to ask.

Modeled Writing

It doesn't matter what grade we're talking about. Students need to see us writing. They need to see us demonstrate the writing process—from the beginning stages where we determine our topic to the final piece. They need to "see" what goes on in our head before our pen hits the paper.

We begin by showing them how we get an idea to write about. We show them how to narrow the topic. In most cases, it doesn't work to just write about "My Cat." A great student-written story often comes from just one particular event: the way Whiskers loves warm laundry, the time she answered the phone when no one was home, the afternoon she couldn't be found, the way she loves "people tuna." After choosing just one of those ideas it's time to show them how to plan the writing (Routman).

Before beginning to write, we talk with them about the particular event so they can see how a story can be made out of it. We think the story out loud with them, put the events in order, and provide enough details so they can "see" the story. Taking the time to do this follows what Katie Wood Ray calls "writing in the air." We encourage them to do a similar thing as they think before they write. Perhaps they might even talk with a friend about what the story might sound like.

After thinking through our story, we show them how to plan it on paper so it is organized. Planning formats can include a list, an outline, a flow chart, or a web. We have found that students often develop a plan and then tuck it away. We show them how their planning page should be right next to their draft so they can see what needs to be included. We make a point of showing how to go from the plan to constructing sentences for a story. It's important to spend enough time initially modeling how to write the complete story from the beginning to the end. Students need to see the planning stage, the decisions we make as we draft our story, and the work that goes into the revising and editing. They need to see the entire writing process.

Using Student Writing in Mini-lessons

We have used students' writings in a number of ways. However, before using any work of a student in the classroom, we get his or her permission first. Some children are very private about their writing and are hesitant to call attention to themselves.

When we notice a student has tried a technique we have been working with, we may want to recognize the attempt and share that with the class. If we notice that a student tried a technique we hadn't yet introduced but saw it in a book he was reading, we may want to point out to others how our reading influences our writing. Sometimes a student wants to try a new technique but isn't sure how to go about it. If the student is willing, you might then use the student's writing in a mini-lesson. By using actual student writing, others in the classroom see that what they struggle with is similar to what others struggle with.

During these mini-lessons, we encourage the student writer to talk about her decisions. Why did she choose such a craft? What was her inspiration? We ask the student to reflect on how well it worked. We also ask her to give some advice to the other student writers who have not tried the technique. And of course, we always have time for the class to ask questions of the student writer.

Jared's writing was used in a mini-lesson to show how he used Dr. Seuss as a mentor author after our Read Across America celebration.

Thinking Through the Typical Writing Workshop Mini-lesson

Whichever method of instruction we choose, we always follow a predictable structure for our mini-lessons. The following will help you in planning and structuring your mini-lessons.

1. **Begin with a connection to and/or review of previous lessons.** How does today's topic fit into your current inquiry unit or how does it specifically address the needs of students? What do students already know and what do they have questions about? Present this brief introduction in a conversational format that avoids leading questions.

2. **Provide a rationale for the lesson.** How will this lesson help your students as writers? Be clear in what you really want the students to pay attention to and why this lesson is important to their writing. Let them know how you expect them to participate in the mini-lesson.

3. **While teaching, continually emphasize the mini-lesson's main topic.** How will your method of instruction impact student writers? During the lesson, stop and share with them what you are thinking. Involve them in the discussion.

4. **In closing the lesson, discuss the possibilities.** How can students use their own words to restate the day's lesson? Keep a record of the lesson on a chart so students can refer to it as needed. How do you want students to connect today's lesson to their own writing? How will you hold them accountable for their application of the instruction? What might the application of the skill look like in your students' writing?

5. **Dismiss writers with a purpose.** Students need a moment or two to gather their thoughts and their ideas before they begin. After the mini-lesson, give some guidance about your expectations of their writing. Prepare your students for their own writing time.

A Recommended Planning Form

This planning form can be especially useful as you begin to plan your mini-lessons. You will soon find that the format becomes very familiar and natural as you deliver your instruction. We have provided a blank template for you and a sample one that is completed so you can see how we might deliver a mini-lesson. This form is not meant to be used as a page in a plan book. It is simply a guide to ensure predictability in your mini-lessons.

In the sample on page 66, our students were already familiar with a circle story structure. However, we weren't seeing this in their writing as much as we would have liked. We knew we needed to model for students how to use such a story structure in order for them to do it for themselves.

Thinking Through Your Mini-lesson

Mini-lesson topic: _____

Unit topic: _____

Literature selections (if applicable): _____

Date: _____

- **Introduction and/or rationale:**

- **Method of lesson delivery:** ☐ Read-aloud ☐ Modeled writing ☐ Shared student writing

- **Teacher notes for lesson:**

- **Discuss the possibilities:**

- **Dismiss writers with a purpose:**

Thinking Through Your Mini-lesson

Mini-lesson topic: *(What one aspect of writing do you wish to discuss or point out to your students today? How does this topic fit into your more general current organizing theme for writing instruction?)*

Unit topic: _____

Literature selections (if applicable): _____

Date: _____

■ **Introduction and/or rationale:**

(Immediately let students "in on" why they are gathered as a group of writers today. Why do good writers need to think about the lesson topic? How will it impact each writer's individual writing pieces?)

■ **Method of lesson delivery:** ☐ Read-aloud ☐ Modeled writing ☐ Shared student writing

(What is the most effective way to deliver this instruction? Will you use a read-aloud and class discussion, or a read-aloud where you point out something you find notable? Is it more appropriate for you to model a kind of writing skill that you had previously talked about in other lessons? Or, is there a piece of student writing that you could share to best convey the mini-lesson topic? Also, how will the students participate in the instruction?)

■ **Teacher notes for lesson:**

(How do you envision the instruction happening? If this lesson is to be mostly teacher-directed, is there a phrase you could repeat over and over during the lesson to help make the topic "stick" in students' heads? If this is to be a discussion-based mini-lesson, what leading questions will you ask to help frame the conversation? If you will be modeling writing, what will you be writing about?)

■ **Discuss the possibilities:**

(How can the students use their own words to restate the day's lesson? Imagine with your class how this particular mini-lesson might affect student writing. Share some "what-ifs" about student writing currently happening in the room. Ask students to share some ways they see the topic or technique enhancing their own writings.)

■ **Dismiss writers with a purpose:**

(What will you say to focus all writers on the immediate writing task at hand? Will you give your students a brief moment to think about their own personal writing and about what they will work on as soon as they return to seats? Will you require that students try out something they learned in the mini-lesson? What can you say to quickly and efficiently transition students from mini-lesson to independent writing?)

▲ *This form is designed to help you understand how to structure mini-lessons.*

Thinking Through Your Mini-lesson

Mini-lesson topic: Using a circle story pattern in student writing

Unit topic: What can we learn from authors?

Literature selections (if applicable):

Date:

■ **Introduction and/or rationale:**

"We've been talking about different ways that authors structure their stories. What do we already know about circular story structures? What stories are you familiar with that use a circular story structure? You know so much about them, I know many of you are ready to write your own story with a circular structure. This is a pattern that could make a lot of our stories even more interesting to our audiences."

■ **Method of lesson delivery:** ☐ Read-aloud ☑ Modeled writing ☐ Shared student writing

"Today I am going to show you how I plan a story with a circular story structure. As I write my plan, I especially want you to notice how my story will begin and how I will plan to have it end. I will not be writing the whole story today—just planning it."

■ **Teacher notes for lesson:**

"As I plan my story I first need to make a list of what I want to include." (Teacher writes and talks in front of students.) "I think I have all the events listed that I want in my story. So now I need to keep in mind that my story's beginning and ending have to match somewhat." (Teacher shows how the beginning thought and the ending thought match.)

■ **Discuss the possibilities:**

"Who can help us give a name to what we did today so we can put it on the chart to help us with our writing?" (Student's response: "Circular Story Plan.") "Let's keep this plan up so you can see how we planned a circular story. We'll keep it near the one we did on a linear story so you can compare them." "When you are writing, how can you apply what we have just talked about to your own writing?" "If you are not writing a circular story structure now, when can this lesson help you?"

■ **Dismiss writers with a purpose:**

"In your writing today, be sure to check and see that you have a clear story structure. If you are writing a circle story, have you thought about the beginning and the end as carefully as I have? And with all your writing, be sure you are using your plans for your story."

▲ *Here is a completed form to show the structure of a mini-lesson from introducing the topic to dismissal.*

Strengthening the Mini-lesson

The correct delivery of instruction strengthens a mini-lesson. But a strong mini-lesson also allows a clear way for students to participate in the lesson. The transition to independent writing is the final piece of the mini-lesson. Students either use this time to assimilate what was just learned into the background knowledge, or they use this time to talk about the day's lunch menu. Again, the teacher must direct this activity.

Student Responsibility During the Mini-lesson

Although the teacher is actively involved in the mini-lesson, the students are not merely passive listeners. We get our students involved by sharing good literature so they not only hear good writing, but they see what the author did to craft his work. When teaching about leads in a story, we pull several books to show varied ways authors begin their books. When we discuss writing in a back-and-forth story structure, we have examples of books that use a similar format as well as books constructed in other structures we discussed previously so they can see the difference.

When we model writing lessons for our students, we involve them in some of our own decision-making. Should I begin a new paragraph here? Did I spell that word correctly? Should this story include dialogue? Should the setting of the story be changed? The students become invested in the lesson and start to take ownership of the story. The idea then seems more doable as they approach their individual writing task.

Ending the Mini-lesson and Connecting It to Student Writing

As we end the mini-lesson, we want our students to think about what they have just learned and how they might be able to apply this to their own writing. We want them to leave the mini-lesson reflecting on what we just discussed. We realize that the day's lesson may not be appropriate for every child on that particular day. However, we can still send them off with a mission, with something to think about in their own writing. "What did we talk about today that might affect what you are working on?" "What can you take from today's lesson to help you in your writing?" "Stop and really do some thinking and ask yourself some tough questions about your writing." "As I meet with students today, I'll be looking for some writing that we can bring to share time. Let's get started."

Older writers may be required to keep a record of the mini-lesson main ideas either in their writing folders or notebooks. After discussing the mini-lesson these students can record what they have learned that day. This way they have a handy reference of the lesson and you have some leverage when a student tells you in his writing conference that he's never heard about adding 's to show possession, even though he has the mini-lesson notes to prove otherwise!

Making a Transition to Independent Writing

Of course, we can't just have the students make a mad dash for their desks and writing folders. We want them to make a smooth transition from our instruction to their independent writing time. We establish a routine and stick to it. Also, we consider our room arrangement and the storage of writing folders and materials.

We have found several successful ways to send students off to their writing areas.

- If students keep their writing folders in their desks, we dismiss them individually or in small groups.

- If students need to get their writing folders from a central location, we send those who have red folders first, then blue folders, and so on. If folders are all the same color, then we dismiss by girls with tennis shoes, boys with khaki pants, and so on.

- If we are rewarding positive behavior, then we send students to get their writing folders because of their good behaviors. "Ashley was so attentive to the mini-lesson. You can get your folder. Michael and Sam look ready to get started. Please get your folders and go quietly to your seats."

- If we have a crate with student writing folders at the meeting area, we hand them out one by one to students who go off to their work areas.

Students need to see that the room is calm and quiet and conducive to getting involved in their writing. When students transition well to the next part of the Workshop, we praise them. When someone needs some redirection, we take care of it before getting involved with student conferences. Our students want the room to feel like a writing environment, just like we do.

CHAPTER 6

Establishing the Workshop
With Procedural Mini-lessons

MUCH OF THE SUCCESS WE SEE IN OUR YOUNG WRITERS COMES FROM THE SHEER AMOUNT OF WRITING THAT THEY DO. We write every day—from the very first day of school to the very last. Even on those rare days when crazy schedules take priority due to things like assemblies or school pictures, we still find time to fit in Writing Workshop. Our writing time quickly becomes a favorite time that students eagerly anticipate. And they let us know they don't approve of schedules that do not include a Writing Workshop. We don't really think this attachment to the writing time stems from the fact that we have so many eager, truly talented, destined to be best-selling authors. We attribute our students' love of writing to something much simpler—our students love to talk about themselves and the things that matter to them. Writing Workshop is a very personal time. Our students grow as writers because they write about what matters to them. They grow as writers because they understand that what is being taught in mini-lessons can actually help them communicate their own thoughts and feelings. They grow as writers because they hold great responsibility in their Writing Workshops.

As you might imagine, we can't just hand over this responsibility to our students without setting down a great deal of ground rules at the beginning. We try our best to help students see their important role in the Writing Workshop from the very first day. We say to the first grader who has never written independently before, "You try it. Write the sounds you hear. You are the author and this is your book." We hope that the young writer hears, "This is my time. My teacher believes I can do this. I am an author!" Yet, at the same time, we can only give so much latitude in the very beginning. Bad habits can be hard to break, so we work very diligently in the beginning months to ensure we establish clear expectations for good habits and allow plenty of time to practice these habits under the watchful eye of the writing teacher.

Creating the Comfort Zone

Our students feel safe to take risks and to trust their own instincts as communicators only to the extent that they feel safe in the classroom environment. The most surefire way to ensure this safety for our children is to wrap them in a routine that very, very rarely changes.

Our Writing Workshops have such a routine. It's simple, and the subtleties change throughout the year, but all in all, the routine remains static—*mini-lesson* to *independent writing time* to *share time*. This structure is in place in every Workshop, every day, from the first Workshop to the last. It is through this predictable routine that we foster a climate of inquiry, communication, writing, and celebration.

We teach procedural mini-lessons mainly at the beginning of the year. However there are always reasons throughout the year to spend some mini-lesson time on procedures. Procedural mini-lessons are not taught in exactly the same way our content lessons are taught. In lessons about craft or conventions, we spend a great deal of time discovering and discussing with the students. In procedural lessons, we spend most of the time telling students how things will progress. Of course, we'll ask if there's agreement, and there are times when we've had to revise our thinking about a certain procedure. But mostly, we use the time in a procedural mini-lesson to set clear expectations for our Writing Workshop.

We dive in at the beginning of each year in a relatively predictable way. We set the tone and the expectations in the same way each year. And so, we've collected a group of lessons that can be used to launch the Writing Workshop. Not all students will need each of these mini-lessons, and some students will need you to go slower, teaching one topic for a couple of days. The following lessons are presented as a guide to beginning your Workshop. These lessons make up the beginning lessons of the first inquiry unit of the year, "How will we become writers in our room?" For each lesson, we provide a possible topic and rationale, as well as supportive teacher talk and other notes that are helpful in elaborating on the message of each procedural mini-lesson.

Good Read-alouds to Accompany Beginning Procedural Mini-lessons

- The Amelia books—Marissa Moss
- *The Art of Reading*—Reading Is Fundamental with a foreword by Leonard S. Marcus
- *Arthur Writes a Story*—Marc Brown
- *Author, a True Story*—Helen Lester
- *Author Talk*—Leonard S. Marcus
- *The Day Eddie Met the Author*—Louise Borden
- *The Day of Ahmed's Secret*—Florence Parry Heide and Judith Heide Gilliland
- *From Pictures to Words*—Janet Stevenson
- *Have You Ever Done That?*—Julie Larios
- *Hey World, Here I Am*—Jean Little
- *If You Were a Writer*—Joan Lowry Nixon
- *Imagine*—Alison Lester
- *Love That Dog*—Sharon Creech
- *A Splendid Friend, Indeed*—Suzanne Bloom
- *What Do Authors Do?*—Eileen Christelow
- *What Do Illustrators Do?*—Eileen Christelow
- *When I Was Your Age* (Vols. 1 and 2)—Amy Ehrlick (ed.)
- Author series by Richard C. Owens—titles include

Best Wishes—Cynthia Rylant	*A Letter From Phoenix Farm*—Jane Yolen
Can You Imagine?—Patricia McKissack	*My Writing Day*—Frank Asch
Firetalking—Patricia Polacco	*Once Upon a Time*—Eve Bunting
From Paper Airplanes to Outer Space—Seymour Simon	*Tell Me a Story*—Jonathan London

Students write a lot in the Writing Workshop. Storing all their work in an organized and helpful way is no small matter. We've had the most success using both individual two-pocket student folders and hanging file folders that house the "portfolio." The folder remains in the student's desk. The draft that is "in production" lives here, as do other drafts that were never finished. We also keep conference notes, mini-lesson notes, spelling guides or resource pages and personal writing goals in this folder.

Twenty Days of Mini-lessons to Build a Strong Writing Workshop

Day 1

Workshop Introduction

Hit the ground writing. From the first day, you want writers to know they will write—for the whole time. Strive to set a positive tone that, hopefully, encourages students to try something, anything at all at this point!

This is a very special part of our day. I'm only going to do a little bit of the talking. You are going to have most of the time to work on things that are important to you. You'll choose what to write about and how to make it better. We'll work together to learn things about how authors craft their work.

With your writing time today, just go make a book or write something, anything—that's appropriate for school. I'll be around to see what amazing things are in your head right now. When you hear (ending signal), *begin the wrap up and place your writing in your new writing folder. I do not expect you to be finished. Then come back and meet me at the carpet.*

Even though you haven't yet addressed any specifics, have students leave this mini-lesson and go write. When you feel there's been enough writing for the first day, have students place their work in their new writing folders. Call students back to you and try to approximate a share time. "Well, what do you think? How did it go? What are you thinking or feeling right now? Would anyone like to tell us what you worked on today? Does anyone know what they might work on tomorrow?"

Day 2

Introduction to the Workshop Schedule and Its Three Main Parts

Make students aware of how your Workshop will run each day. Refer to a written schedule with approximate times. Help students begin to feel comfortable with the expectation that no Workshop time should be wasted. Use this lesson to make students aware of how you will transition from one part of the Workshop to another. The more they know, the smoother it will go.

Take a look at our writing schedule. We'll start each day here in a Writers' Meeting (or mini-lesson). Then I will dismiss a few of you at a time to go back to your writing spots (usually just their seats) and begin working in your writing folder. I'll give you a chance to start writing, and then I will begin talking with individuals in writing conferences. Some days, I might ask a small group to come meet me at the group table. Everyone will write and work until I ring the bell. When you hear the bell, please come to a stopping point, clean up, and meet us all back at the meeting area. We'll spend that share time talking about what you accomplished during writing time.

In the younger grades, we often practice just the movement of this schedule a few times on this day. We meet, get up, pretend to work quietly for a while, listen for the bell, and then return to the meeting area. It would not be uncommon for a first grade class to dry-run through these steps three or four times. Smooth transitions make for much Workshop success.

Using the Writing Center

Day 3

This lesson will mean various things in various classrooms. It will look very different in different grade levels. But whatever the classroom, this lesson aims to acquaint students with the tools and materials they have at their disposal during the Writing Workshop. During this lesson, you should go over, in great detail, the inner workings of the "writing center." You'll need to cover where this writing center is located, what is in the writing center, what students can (and should) do on their own, and what they might need assistance with. You'll also need to lay out your expectations for how it is to be kept and who will be responsible for it. (Though all students should always be respectful of materials, we've found it helpful to rotate the job of "Writing Center Patrol" to clean up the area at Workshop's end.) This lesson may include where finished products should go, how to assemble books, how to inform you of missing or depleted supplies, or even how to use the stapler correctly. It often stretches into two or more mini-lessons, depending on how much needs to be covered.

While we know that an author's most powerful tools are the words he uses, writers often need a great deal of materials to write an interesting book (or piece). We are going to have all of the tools you will require as an author, and we're going to keep them in a special place, "the writing center." Today we'll take a careful look at our writing center and how you'll be expected to use it.

Beginning to Write— Modeled Writing

Day 4 **Day 5**

No matter how old our students are, they need to see all that our writing expectations entail.

In the upper grades, use this lesson to think aloud how you might select a topic and begin mapping out the ideas for the piece. On the second day, show students (on the overhead machine, using the same sort of paper available to them) how to use plans from the previous day to begin writing. You'll model your thinking as you go, editing as you go, and rereading for clarity, even though these components aren't the main focus of the lesson. You probably won't bring your piece to final copy;

you're not there yet in the Workshop. You want to help these students begin and keep writing the entire time. You want to help them believe they have something to write about, even if it doesn't look polished.

In the lower grades, the topic of the first mini-lesson will be, "Yes, you can spell it without me. Say the word very slowly and write down the sounds you hear." You'll write only about one or two sentences in front of them, emphasizing how we can say a word and record the sounds.

In the second lesson, you'll focus on the book making. You can model how to select and create a book. Think aloud about how you choose a topic, how you fill up the pages of the book using details, and how you know the book is finished (or not finished).

So far, I have seen some interesting ideas popping up out there as you write. I want to take a few minutes to show you what I might do if I were writing in this Writing Workshop. As you watch me, think to yourself, "How can I do something like that?"

Day 6

Helping Yourself in the Writing Workshop— Introducing and Creating Resources

Creating self-sufficient writers helps to ensure that you'll be able to work with individual writers with little interruption. Many young writers think that as soon as they don't know how to spell a word, they've come to a stopping point (a bad habit to break quickly!). Resources in the classroom and the expectation that students solve problems on their own go a long way to eliminate this "writer's block." In the upper grades, you'll use this time to refresh (or teach) dictionary and thesaurus skills or to refer students to word walls, other books in the classroom, and other spelling devices. In the primary years, you'll focus mostly on using the word walls and books in the classroom. You may also want to create word lists to post near the word wall. For example, because so many young writers choose to write about their families and lives at home, we make a large "person" cutout, call him the "Family Man," and together with the class, fill him with all the words about our families that we think we might need.

Sometimes young writers think that not being able to spell a word is the end of the world. Not being able to spell is a simple problem with lots of possible solutions. In our Writing Workshop, not being able to spell a word is never a reason to stop working. Let's think together of all the ways we could solve this very common problem.

What can you do when you can't spell a word?

- Don't just sit there! Do something.

- Say it slowly and write the sounds you hear.

- Think of another word you know that sounds like it.

- Clap out the parts.

- Check the dictionary.

- Check the word wall.

- Ask a friend.

- Give it a try and circle it. Talk to your teacher about it when you conference.

Helping Yourself in the Writing Workshop— Teacher Modeling

Day 7

Whatever expectations or introductions you make the day or days before, students are going to need some time to digest this information and to see just exactly how those resources can help them. Perhaps your students need more practice with the skill of using electronic spelling resources. Perhaps you want them to practice locating and copying words from the word wall. Perhaps you think your students would benefit from watching you use a resource while you're in the middle of writing and thinking. By devoting another day's mini-lesson time to the use of resources in the room, you are again emphasizing the fact that students are expected to be thinkers and problem-solvers in the Workshop.

Yesterday we began talking about what to do if you get stuck on a word. Let's review yesterday's chart. Remember, this chart will be up all year in case you forget or need another way to solve your problem.

Today I'm going to show you how I might use some of these resources during writing time. Pay careful attention to when and how I get up to use these resources.

Because we want to avoid stopping to find a word and then forgetting all about the rest of the thought, we try to model indicating a spelling approximation with a small dot above a questionable word. We return to that word after we have written the complete thought that was in our head.

Get your ideas out and lightly mark the word you're unsure of. Write something, any sounds you hear, for the word. Come back to the word and use your resources when you've written your whole thought. Sometimes our thoughts are slippery and they slip right out of our heads. Don't let that happen because of a tricky word!

Strengthening Share Time—An Introduction

Day 8

By now, your students are working hard during independent writing. It may not be the best writing, but they are practicing what it feels like to be a writer. There's one more component of the Workshop that needs to be addressed—share time. In the last couple of days, you've met again as a class after Independent Writing. You've talked about what went well, and you've troubleshot things that weren't working. But the great potential of share time has yet to be realized. And once again, you've got to lead students slowly through the hows and the expectations. On this day, plan to meet writers for a very brief mini-lesson time. Have them do their independent writing, but close it up earlier than you would normally. For these share time lessons, you'll want to do the majority of teaching at the share time gathering. This way, the continuity and routine will not be altered.

We're going to do something a bit different today. Instead of having our talk before our writing time, we're going to have a longer talk after our writing time.

When we meet then, we're going to talk about how our share time should look.

At the end of every Workshop, we'll have a chance to come together again as writers to celebrate our successes, help each other over hurdles, and learn from the other authors in the room. Sometimes I will be asking you during independent writing time if you'd share what you're working on. Other times, you might feel you need some help or that you've really done a fabulous crafting job and you can bring something to share on your own. Remember, we might not get to everyone each day. But over time, you will all have a chance to share.

What are your thoughts and questions about share time?

This would be your chance to reinforce a strong foundation of expectations. If a student brings up something that you hadn't thought of, great! Think it over and have an answer ready tomorrow. Help the student see that he or she has a hand in creating the Workshop.

Day 9   Day 10

Strengthening Share Time—Modeling and Guided Practice

As with any expectation you set out for students, it's best to show them exactly what you mean. This lesson will take place at share time. Spend your time during independent reading finding students who will be able to share and model appropriate work. For example, highlight a student who independently solved a problem or a student who is using time wisely and has lots of detail to show for it. At share time, invite these students up, one at a time.

I've noticed that a few of our authors are meeting with great success. Let's take a moment and see what we can learn from others in our room. Make sure that when you are the listener, you are listening carefully. If you are the speaker, make sure that the whole class can hear you. When the speaker is finished sharing, I'll ask you what you noticed about their work, and we'll talk about how it might be able to help other authors.

This ongoing chart records lessons learned from other students at share time. ▶

My Writing Friends

We learned	from our friend...
to have an idea for each page	Montrel
we can try a new kind of book	Olivia
to think about the books we read	Xavier, Michael T
books need a beginning, middle and end	James Chris
Books can repeat.	Kiyaijzia
Authors can write how they got the idea	Brooklin

Day 11 — Strengthening Share Time—Learning From One Another

Share time is most powerful when it becomes another form of instruction. In the previous lessons on share time, you focused mostly on *what* this time is. In this lesson, you'll want to focus on the *how* of share time. This happens when you carefully steer the discussion after each "sharer."

Wow, Emily, I loved how you told us so many details about how your bedroom looked. I feel as if I were there. I'm wondering if what Emily has done successfully would help anyone else's writing become stronger. How might you use lots of details in your story about Christmas dinner, Jared? Is there anyone else who can think of a way that adding details might help the story they are writing? Thanks, again, Emily for showing us how adding many details helps readers to visualize your story.

Day 12 — Appropriate Workshop Voices

One more big management issue that needs to be addressed during these beginning lessons is the issue of noise in the room. It's not expected that the independent writing room be silent. Writers need to feel secure in the fact that they have the option to talk to a friend about an unknown word or an idea they are stuck on. However, there's a fine line between productive chatter and just plain noise.

We know that we will write together, that we'll be able to help each other along the writing process. In order to do this we need to be able to talk to one another. We don't always need to talk though. And, it's very important that you remember all the talking you are allowed to do during writing time must be about your writing. We are going to allow strong "writer's talk," not everyday talk. Let's talk about what this may look like and sound like in our writing room.

Spend some time in discussion with your students. We found a T-chart that lists what "Writer's Talk" looks like and sounds like to be the best way to address and illustrate our concerns and our need to set up the best possible writing environment.

Writers' Talk in our Workshop. In the lower grades, it is very helpful to have students draw pictures of what this means to them. These pictures are often powerful reminders when students need to be redirected throughout the year.

What strong talk looks like...

- Writers talking close together, not from across the room
- Referring to books—our own or other authors'
- Referring to charts
- One person talking while the other person listens carefully; taking turns
- Friends being helpful and kind to one another
- Writers are looking at some type of writing

What strong talk sounds like...

- Using a whisper voice—a voice that others cannot hear
- Using manners and kind, helpful words about others' writing
- One writer offering suggestions, not just telling what to do
- Discussions about the writing process and nothing else

What can I write about?

Day 13

By now, many students are getting over the initial excitement of writing about whatever they want and fall into the "What should I write about?" slump. They need a little more guidance with topic selection. (This is just a brief introduction. Many classes study topic selection for quite a while after the procedural lessons are all complete.) This lesson is where we begin to set the foundation that throughout our writing studies, we will learn about writing from writers. To get the discussion going, pull a collection of books you've already read together that seem to have been written for a variety of reasons. Begin by asking, "How might the author have gotten this idea?"

Let's take a look at some of our favorite books we've read together, and let's speculate about how we think the author got the idea for the book.

Begin a reference chart, "Writers get ideas . . ." Often we find it important to point out that writers write about what they truly care about, what they've just gotta write about, and things that are so interesting, they know other readers need to know about. Early in the year, we help our writers to see that their best writing most often comes out of their strongest feelings. Ideas don't work just because they worked for someone else in the room.

Modeled Thinking and Writing— Using the Writing Process

Day 14 Day 15

All students are well into the routine of the Workshop, and they should now realize that there are expectations for how they are to use their time. It's time to return to the idea of how the writing process will help them as writers. It's imperative that we show them exactly what we mean. When modeling, tell what you are thinking, don't just show the words that appear on your paper. It's also important to be sure what you are modeling matches the expectations you have for your students. In first grade, we expect one thought on each page and about four or five pages early in the year. When we model, we'll make a book (just a bit bigger so all can see), and we'll write one thought on each page, with about five pages in our book. In fourth grade, we're expecting at least a few sentences on each page. That's exactly what we'll model for them.

We're going to take some time to see just what happens during the writing process. I'm going to show you how I think of a topic, plan for my writing, write my thoughts, and then reread to be sure my writing is ready for others to read. As I do this, I want you to pay close attention to how I am thinking and planning as I write. When you notice me doing something that you could do as a writer, let's stop to talk about that.

Day 16

Modeled Writing— Rereading and Adding On

One of the main ideas that gets repeated continuously throughout all of our Workshops is the idea that "Writers revise." We need to show our students, even at these very beginning stages, the importance of rereading and possibly saying even more. Eventually we'll talk about taking some ideas out, checking for punctuation and spelling, and choosing more descriptive words. For now, though, we simply need our students to begin to slow it down just a bit. To begin this journey of self-reflection, our students need to see exactly what it entails. We model rereading our work and adding in some details. We introduce the importance of revision.

I'm going to take another look at the book I've been writing the last couple of days. It is most important for writers to go back to what they've already written. I'll be listening to what my book sounds like. Sometimes I forget to put in little words that need to be there. As I reread, I'm going to ask myself, "Is there anything else I should tell my readers so that my readers can see what I am seeing?" Listen and watch carefully. When you get to your own writing today, I'm going to ask you to look over your work. See if you can add on or change the way I am doing now.

Day 17

Setting "All Done!" Criteria

This lesson piggybacks on the previous lessons in that we use it to give our writers a framework and a reminder about rereading their work. Another chart that you'll create and use throughout the year is titled "My piece (or book) is finished when . . ." This is yet another opportunity you have for reinforcing your expectations. We'll start in the beginning with simple things such as, "I'm finished when my name is on it and I have reread it." Or, in older grades, "I'm finished when I have a clear beginning, middle, and end." As the year progresses and we learn more and more about what writers do, we can add to this list. We keep this chart posted right above the finished folders. Students have to check and see if they are truly finished before filing the story away.

I've noticed that many of you are coming to the end of your writing and getting right up and filing your writing away. I'm proud of the way you keep on writing, but I'm concerned that

"Teacher to Teacher"

We see a difference between finished work and published work. Most of the work our students turn in is finished. It may be the final draft that is complete with editing and revision, but it may not be copy perfect. (Let's face it. We know that even if we asked a student to copy his work over three times to get it perfect, we would get three different versions all with different mistakes.)

❦

In the beginning of the year, we notice students coming to the last page of their book—or running out of steam after a few pages—and simply writing, "The end," even though there was nothing in the "plot" to suggest it really was the end. We like to take a week or so and do a mini-inquiry called "The End is not really the end." Over a couple of days, we read books and focus on the endings, seeing if we can find other, interesting ways to end our books. We find books that end by repeating the first page, books that seem to suggest there's more to come at the end, books that end with a question, and books that clearly have a release, a happy ending. After taking even this brief look at how stories can end, students understand the need for a strong ending and possess a few strategies for how to go about this. Of course, this mini-inquiry would end with a day or two of teacher modeling how to incorporate an ending into a story.

many of you are not taking the time to check and be sure you are truly finished with the piece. Let's talk about what it means to be finished with a piece of writing. Let's begin a reminder chart that you must refer to before putting your writing away. This will help us to think about how each book we write will be better than the book before it because we are really taking the time to look over our writing before starting a new piece.

"All Done!"

My writing is ready to go in the finished bin when . . .

- I have read and reread it to myself.

- I have read it to someone else.

- My friend can understand my handwriting.

- I can see my name and the title on the cover.

- I am sure I've written a beginning, middle, and end.

- I can say how it is better than my last book.

- I have used lots of effort.

- I am proud of my work.

▲ *The look of these "All Done!" charts change across grade levels. We start the year with only one or two criteria listed. As we learn new things about writing, we continue to add to this chart. By year's end, all grade level expectations for writing will be listed on the chart.*

"I'm All Done. Now What?"

We need to be clear to our students that we expect them to keep up the writing momentum. Students need to know where to put pieces that are finished. They need to know how to begin work on a new piece without your assistance each time. They need to understand that "I'm done!" is never an option in the Writing Workshop.

Writers, now that we've taken a really close look at all the things we need to think about before considering a piece finished, we're ready to answer the "What's Next?" question. I want to show you today how to file your finished pieces in the finished bin. I also want you to watch how I move from the finished bin right into thinking about a new piece to write about.

You may want to show them how you return to your seat and just think for a minute, how you might reread the chart on where writers get ideas, how you might just start writing a few things down. You'll want to show them how you can, fairly quickly, begin a new piece. Few students will be able to follow exactly in your footsteps at this point. But, they will know where to put finished pieces. And they will know we expect them to keep going. They'll know they are never "All Done!"

Choosing Appropriate Topics

Day 19

Students are now used to the routine of writing each day. They are beginning to see that they really are in charge of what to write about. We need to start having some conversations about what is appropriate and what is not. Often in the younger grades, it's enough for us to say that we do not want to see writing about TV, movies, games, or toys. Up until this point, we have allowed such topics because we were more interested in everybody actually writing. In the upper grades, it's best to be more clear about inappropriate content. We ask our students to consider whether their topic/piece would be one that we would choose to read aloud to the class. If the answer is no, then it should not be written in the Writing Workshop.

Writers, now that we're really coming to understand that authors choose topics they truly care about, I think it's time we set up some rules for what we are going to write about. From today on, we should not write about TV shows, movies, toys, or other games. Please think about topics that really matter to you and ideas that don't belong to other people.

Writing Workshop in Our Classroom—A Review

On this last lesson of Workshop setup, we ask our students to take a look back over all the charts and writings we have done together. We ask them to retell what Writing Workshop is to them and what they need to do to keep it moving smoothly. We make a big deal of saying, "Now we're ready for the good stuff of writing."

Writers, I am so proud of all the hard work you have done setting up our Writing Workshop. Let's take another look at what our jobs are, what you expect and what I expect of our Writing Workshop time.

Different classes record this conversation in different ways. Some classes write a pledge for their Workshop, and others chart a list of rules and responsibilities. In some classrooms, students do a creative response titled "Writing Workshop Is . . ." What matters is that students clearly understand that the ground rules have been set and that the writers in the room are expected to play by these rules for the remainder of the school year.

During these beginning mini-lessons, we use the mini-lesson and share time to tell students what we expect them to do and show how they are expected to do it. In the beginning, during independent writing time, the majority of our time is spent troubleshooting. It would not be uncommon to see a teacher remaining in the writing center just after her students have learned to use it. We use this time to make sure students are not acquiring bad habits. We often hear from teachers that this seems like an awfully long time to spend just "fixing up" the Workshop. These teachers are concerned about not "instructing" students in the specifics of writing. It's a leap of faith, true, but the time you spend on these details in September and early October will allow you to reap great rewards later in the year. Your students' work will reflect the care you've taken to ensure a strong, secure writing environment for your writers and thinkers.

Sample Procedural Mini-lesson

Portfolio Selection Procedures

A couple of times throughout the year, our students review their writing portfolios and clean out all but their best pieces. We prepare them to self-reflect and make judgments. In this mini-lesson, we help students think about how to make choices and exactly what to do when these choices are made. There's a lot a paper flying around when 20 or more students spread out across the room and go through all of their writing. If we're not clear about what to do, the room can quickly become chaotic.

In preparation for this lesson and activity, Marybeth has placed a large brown envelope on each student's desk and a star stamp and ink pad at each table.

Writers, today is a very important day in our Writing Workshop. Our writing portfolios are busting out of their crates! We need to take a look at all the writing we have done in the last few weeks and think about what you should keep here and what can go home. Before we do this, I want to talk with you about how best to do this and show you exactly what you'll need to do when you make your selections.

Marybeth has already thought this one through. She comes to the mini-lesson with a chart (right). In primary grades, there would be picture clues on the chart.

I've already made a helper chart. We're all going to be doing the same thing today. Let's take a look. First I need you to get your writing portfolio file folder and find a quiet, private space where you will work all by yourself. You'll also need a little room to spread out. Next, think about where you will put three different piles. You're going to read each piece of writing and decide if it's great, OK, or not that great. Then you'll put it in the correct pile.

For younger students, we actually give them a picture of thumbs up, thumbs sideways, and thumbs down. This way, they have a place for their piles and they are less apt to get their piles confused.

When you've read all your pieces, look at the great pile only. Now, you have to pick the two best from this pile. Take these two pieces over to the table and put a star stamp on each piece. This way we'll know they were your best pieces of the first quarter. Put these pieces back into the file folder. Finally, go back and take all of your other writing and put it into the big brown envelope. You'll take that home to show your family.

Let's go back to the chart and think about this again.

Selecting Best Pieces From My Portfolio

- Private space
- Make three piles: Great!, OK, Definitely not my best
- Read and sort
- Pick two
- Star stamp
- File folder
- Brown envelope

She does a quick recap of each bullet, asking if anything is unclear.

Now, writers, I want you to watch me as I try to do just what I've asked you to do. Use the helper chart and help me, OK?

Marybeth prepares to model and think aloud her actions for each direction. She makes some intentional mistakes and asks students to keep checking the direction chart for her. As a final step, she asks a few students to use their own words and say just what they are to do.

All right, writers, when I call your name, come up and get your portfolio. Go find a thinking spot and remember to keep checking the chart.

Such a mini-lesson drastically differs from other mini-lessons about craft or even writing skills. We don't save a lot of room for student input. In a procedural lesson, we typically come knowing what we want. (Or, if this is the first time we're trying something, what we think we want.) The directions of this lesson may seem like overkill. However, we know from experience that because of the generally loose atmosphere in the Writing Workshop, it doesn't take much to spin out of control. This will not happen on a typical day when students know exactly what to do and what to expect. But, on the days where you are trying something new like portfolio selection, you must hold tight to the reins. A procedural mini-lesson that includes a reference for directions, clear explanations of the directions, teacher modeling and, finally, student retelling of the direction may seem laborious. However, success is practically guaranteed. And, if we have to switch things up a bit and, every once in a while, hold a teacher-directed, "because I said so" lesson in order to maintain the peace and our sanity, then so be it!

Studying Audience

HEN WE FIRST SAT DOWN AND STARTED TO DISCUSS HOW WE MIGHT BRING THE IDEA OF "AUDIENCE" TO OUR YOUNG WRITERS WE HAD MIXED FEELINGS. Did we really want our students to think that lots of people would be reading all of their work? Would they feel safe enough to take risks if this audience was always looking over their shoulders? Can young egocentric students truly understand this idea of someone else? Yet, in deference to all of our other successes, there was no other way to tackle these concerns than to just dive in and see what happened.

As it turns out, young authors are not at all put off by the idea of audience, and they are able to recognize the benefits of always considering the audience. Perhaps most important though, we found an awesome and realistic way to "sneak in" lessons about writing conventions, grammar, and legibility—all under the guise of, "You need to do what's best for your audience." No longer do our students put in commas because we tell them to. They think about such conventions as their own responsibility. And we are sure to tell them over and over again, "Your readers are counting on you to help them understand your message."

Making "Audience" Accessible to Students

We have had success with books such as *Curious George Goes to the Ballet* by Margret Rey and Alan J. Shalleck and *Honk!* by Pamela Edward Duncan to begin our exploration of audience.

"Teacher
to
Teacher"

Perhaps you've come across that one student who will call you on the idea of audience. It's possible for a student to answer your call to think about the audience with, "But no one is really going to read this. I'm really the only audience, and I think it's just fine." To this student, and then to all in the class, we'll admit that, yes, there are times when we are only writing for ourselves (to-do lists, journals, and so on). But if we're not clear, even for ourselves, it's possible to lose the meaning. And if pushed further, we can always remind this student that in our Writing Workshops, there is always another audience besides the writer—the teacher will always want to take a look!

In our classrooms, we begin our discussion of audience by clearly defining what we mean when we, as teachers, say, "Think of your audience." Older children and some younger children may have enough background information to jump right into a discussion. For those students who need a clearer picture of an audience, we usually turn to a read-aloud to build this knowledge. And of course, for better or for worse, no beginning discussion of audience is complete without remembering a trip to the movies!

As a class, we talk about when we have been in an audience and how we act as an audience. We slowly lead the conversation to the idea that an audience requires someone or something to listen to or to focus on. When we write, we are creating something that someone else needs to understand.

Once we're certain that our writers understand what an audience is in general, we talk specifically about how audience pertains to our writing. A writer needs an audience. A writer writes to share her ideas with others. A writer can make an audience change its mind, laugh, cry, or feel a certain way. A writer can make different people feel differently. There's quite a bit of power afforded to the writer in this case. Many students are intrigued by these ideas. To facilitate this conversation, we pull out some of our favorite read-alouds and ask questions such as, "What did Robert Munsch do to make us laugh so hard in this book? . . . But he didn't really want the audience to laugh in this book, did he . . . ?" We nudge our young authors to start thinking beyond the immediate "me." We want our writers to be thinking about why they are writing and how they can make their own thoughts and ideas more accessible to others.

The next step in effectively using the audience to strengthen writing in our classroom is to move from these generalities about audience to specifics. What is it that writers need to do so that their work can be fully enjoyed and understood by their readers, their audience? We come to the next day's mini-lesson with chart paper already titled "My audience needs me to . . ." The charts look different depending on the grade level and the time of year. However, this list will serve as a reminder of all the things that we've asked our writers to think about thus far. It also stays up so that we add to it throughout the year. The following are examples of second-grade and fourth-grade audience charts from halfway through the year:

My audience needs me to . . .

- Think carefully about my handwriting
- Choose interesting topics
- Have a clear beginning, middle, and end
- Remember periods and capital letters
- Put my name on the cover
- Check for spelling errors
- Add details to slow the story down
- Reread to be sure it sounds right

▲ *What Second Graders Think About When Writing for an Audience*

My audience needs me to . . .

- Have a well organized paper that stays on the topic
- Consider my choice of words so my paper is interesting to read
- Elaborate with specific examples and details
- Have a consistent point of view
- Write in complete sentences and vary the sentence structure
- Use proper grammar
- Use appropriate capitalization and punctuation
- Check for spelling
- Write legibly

What Fourth Graders Think About When Writing for an Audience ▶

Generating Topics for an Audience

While most classrooms begin the year with a look at ways to think up writing ideas, we always return to this idea of choosing topics once we've introduced the importance of audience. Many writers write on topics that we personally don't find interesting. The trick is that good writers find something they care enough about so that they will produce strong writing. We ask our writers, "What is it that you really care about that you know you could turn into good writing . . . so that you can make others care about this topic as well?"

Oftentimes, students will write again and again about their friends. The writing is often superficial and repetitive. Once our students know about writing for an audience, our conversations about such pieces become more pointed, more helpful. We can now tell these writers that just saying, "I like my friend Tom. We have fun when we play. We play at my house and we play at his house. Tom and I have fun when we play," doesn't quite do it for the audience. While we don't want to discourage this author from writing about Tom, we want him to try to look at his piece from the audience's perspective. What might really interest someone about what he and Tom like to do? Was there a really funny thing

"Teacher to Teacher"

An excellent way to help introduce students to thinking about their audience is to offer them nonexamples of what you are talking about. For example, a second-grade teacher wants her students to think about legibility and punctuation. She writes a note to the class in terrible handwriting and no or incorrect punctuation. Although she's very excited to share her writing with her students, the students are unable to read her work. And from there ensues an interesting discussion about what the *teacher did wrong* and what the other authors in the room can learn from her mistakes.

that happened? Scary? Sad? What could he write about that might help others really come to like Tom as well? Again, it's much easier to sit with this writer in a conference and ask, "What might the audience think?" Rather than just saying to the author, "You need to go back and add more interesting details"— words that, to a struggling writer, translate as just another "No, try again." Adding more details is exactly what the teacher in us is going for, but suddenly the onus is off of us, and the responsibility lies with the writer. More details are needed at the insistence of his "audience," not his nagging teacher.

Teaching Writing Skills

Discussing audience also gives the teacher a similar advantage when it comes to the rules of writing—the do's and don'ts involved with grammar, punctuation, and capitalization. While we don't teach all of our grammar objectives during our unit on audience, we do always begin writing skill lessons by reminding our writers to think about how we are always writing to be clear to our audience.

Writers, another way we can help our audience understand our ideas is to be sure we are writing in ways that make sense. There are certain tools writers can use to help them get their message across more clearly. These tools are the rules that all writers follow and that all audiences understand. I'd like to take a close look at one of these tools today and see how we can use it to make our writing even stronger.

As you might expect, such skill lessons are taught as guided inquiry. As with every other aspect of our writing instruction, it's important to us that we do not merely "hand down" writing rules and conventions from "on high." We set up opportunities for students to see and discover how and why things are the way they are. Yes, it takes a bit longer to show a couple of texts that use commas in a series and to ask our writers if they notice something that all three passages have in common. But through this discovery, a deeper understanding is nurtured. Commas in a series will show up consistently in student writing only when the writers have true understanding of such a writing convention. And again, since improving their own writing is our ultimate goal in our Writing Workshops, we feel the time is well spent.

There is a difference between our writing lessons that focus on writer's craft or word choice and our lessons on specific writing conventions. In our lessons about craft, once our students are familiar with how we can look at a text in different ways, we often start the lesson not knowing exactly where we'll end up. Again, we don't have all the answers concerning craft, word choice, and style. However, in writing skill lessons, we do have an answer and know exactly what we want the students to take away from the lesson. We want them to begin following a certain writing rule. For this reason, we present these mini-lessons in predictable ways that vary slightly from the lessons referred to in Chapter 5.

A Predictable Plan for Teaching Writing Conventions and Rules

Steps 1 and 2 contain the planning portion of the lesson, while Steps 3 through 6 provide the steps of the actual mini-lesson.

1. **Choose the convention you need to teach.** We must all teach our required objectives, but whenever possible, the choice should be based on our writers' most immediate needs. Are the majority of writers in the room ready to follow such a rule? When the convention starts to appear around the room, it's a good time to teach how to use it correctly before too many writers start to practice using it incorrectly. (This is often the case with quotation marks, apostrophes, ellipses, and colons.)

2. **Find and gather resources.** In this case, *resources* refers to written material that includes the correct use of the identified topic. We look in all possible places. You can use picture books, chapter books, newspapers, magazines, student writing, your own writing . . . anything at all that shows a clear example of what you are talking about. One thing to think about, though, is the size of the print. If you really want your students to focus on the use of quotation marks, they've got to be able to see the quotation marks during the mini-lesson. It won't really make sense if you just tell them what you are seeing. This visual piece of understanding cannot be overlooked. Big books or overheads work best.

3. **Connect to writing you have seen from authors in the room.** Show them right off the bat that there is a true need for the rule and lead into a lesson about subject-verb agreement.

   Writers, the other day while I was conferring with Alexis, we noticed that something wasn't sounding just right. Her book read, "The sun shine on the flowers. The sun smile on the trees. The sun heat up all the people." After I talked with Alexis, I thought about how other authors might be having the same sort of trouble making the writing sound more like we talk in our classroom.

4. **Share examples and discuss what is noticed.** It's important, while reading, to emphasize the subject and the verb ending, leading students to hear and focus on the lesson objective. Ask for students to begin verbalizing what they notice and steer the discussion accordingly.

   Writers, take a look at this article I found in a sports magazine for kids. Follow along on the overhead as I read a couple of other writing pieces from other authors. See if you can hear how these sentences sound correct. And think about how we might be able to help out Alexis.

5. Determine the rule that all writers will follow. As is often the case, the teacher must restate what the class is saying in order to make the rule or reminder more concise and, for that matter, more helpful. The "rule" that the class settles on does not need to be taken word for word from your grammar book. The rule needs to be accurate and understandable to all in the room. Using students' own words is one more way we help to ensure understanding and mastery.

What I hear most of you saying is that you have to think about the sentence you are writing carefully. You have to think about who is doing what. Sometimes you have to change the end of the action word depending on how many are doing the action. Alexis should change shine *to* shines*: the sun shines. But, two suns would shine. Let me say that again: listen carefully and decide if our rule makes sense. Sometimes you have to change the end of the action word depending on how many are doing the action.*

6. Record the rule for writers to use as a reference. Depending on the grade level, you have a few options with how you record your lesson objective. You can write out the rule and post it with other similar rules you've discovered. Students can record the rule in their writing notebooks or folders. Or you can do both. What's most important here is the expectation that once a rule or reminder is "discovered" and "posted" in your writing classroom, it needs to be implemented in students' writing. Writers are held accountable for including what has been learned in their own writing. Obviously, there is some wiggle room here for your varying needs in the classroom. Some students will not be able to apply such ideas. And some students will need continuous reminders. But all students will have access to the rule and its proper use.

7. Remind, refer, redirect. Such a method of inquiry is only successful to the extent the teacher consistently holds students to these standards. Once it's up, it's expected. Students need to know that just because we talked about inserting dialogue in November, they will still be expected to do it correctly in May. By using their own notes and the reminders you have posted, there's usually less teacher-directed fixing of errors. In a conference in which we see that an author has forgotten a rule we had previously learned, we simply point out that rule in their own notes. Almost without exception, students are able to fix their own errors. This self-correction provides yet another opportunity for in-depth, personal understanding of a writing convention.

Gathering resources for such a lesson is very simple. Since many of the authors we share with our students write in conventional ways, it's very easy to find a few examples of what you'd like to talk about. Perhaps you want to introduce students to the correct use of the semicolon. You might skim through a few picture books to find places where it is used. Magazine articles are bound to have a few. Or, you might visit your grammar guide and simply use the sample sentences given there. Type them up and show them on the overhead. Your examples don't need to show amazing word choice. You just want to afford your students the chance to take a look and see what they notice before you just tell them the rule.

As a side note to this type of instruction, we also present our students with opportunities to practice applying the rules of grammar and writing conventions that they will see on standardized tests. In many of our testing grades, students do a daily five-question quiz to practice using these rules and applying them to someone else's writing. The quizzes are checked each day together with the students. This affords teachers time to teach and reteach rules and conventions.

Two fabulous books to share with your class while looking closely at how authors use punctuation are *Punctuation Takes a Vacation* by Robin Pulver and Lynn Rowe Reed and *Eats, Shoots & Leaves: Why, Commas Really Do Make a Difference!* by Lynne Truss and Bonnie Timmons.

The Importance of Organization and Text Structure

We use correct grammar and agreed-upon writing conventions because our audience expects us to do so. Our audience expects punctuation, capitalization, subject-verb agreement, and the like because that's the way our written language works. As readers, we are thrown when we come across a grammatical error or the misuse of a punctuation mark. (Because of this, writers can purposely manipulate writing conventions to convey a certain feeling.) Our audience can concentrate on the meaning of what we have to say only when our mechanics do not get in the way of comprehension.

Likewise, our audience needs us to structure the writing in a way that makes sense. At its most basic level this means that written pieces typically have a beginning, middle, and end. But there are many other ways that a text can be structured. Readers, because of their "story sense" (knowledge of how stories work), know at a certain level what to expect as a story unfolds. When we read, we know that this author always writes two parallel stories simultaneously or that another author's endings seem to come out of nowhere. By structuring writing in predictable, organized ways, authors help their audience to understand their message. Our young writers need clear instruction that will help them to create well-structured, organized pieces.

You might have a hard time believing this, but discovering and identifying text structure is very exciting to our young writers. It does take some time before students fully understand what they are looking for. But, when they do, they'll have to tell you the structure of every book you will ever read again! We begin to build this understanding at the very beginning, again, through the process of discovery.

A beginning lesson on text structure requires us to have a collection of three or four books with a similar text structure. Usually, students have heard most or all of these selections before. (We don't like to spend the entire mini-lesson reading and rereading from more than one book.) After spending a few minutes rediscovering these texts, we extend our ever-present invitation, "Tell me what you notice . . . what is the same about these three books?"

If we have carefully selected the texts, it should be clear that the stories

Beginning a Study of Text Structure

Here is a list of possible books to choose for the introductory part of the text structure inquiry. The structures in these stories are fairly obvious and relatively easy for students to articulate. Because the task here is simply defining text structure, these books work across grade levels.

Back-and-forth stories:

- *The Blue and the Gray*—Eve Bunting
- *Lost*—Paul Brett Johnson and Celeste Lewis
- *Now I'm Big*—Margaret Miller
- *When I Was Five*—Arthur Howard

Circle stories:

- *Chicka Chicka Boom Boom*—Bill Martin, Jr.
- *The Great Gracie Chase*—Cynthia Rylant
- *My Mama Had a Dancing Heart*—Libba Moore Gray
- *The Paperboy*—Dav Pilkey
- *The Sick Day*—Patricia MacLachlan
- *Watch the Stars Come Out*—Riki Levinson

Letter stories:

- *Dear Levi*—Elvira Woodruff (chapter book)
- *Dear Mr. Blueberry*—Simon James
- *Dear Mr. Henshaw*—Beverly Cleary (chapter book)
- *Dear Peter Rabbit*—Alma Flor Ada
- *Dear Willie Rudd,*—Libba Moore Gray
- *I Wanna Iguana*—Karen Kaufman Orloff
- *Letters From Rifka*—Karen Hesse (chapter book)

Linear stories (problem, events, solution):

- *Baghead*—Jarrett J. Krosoczka
- *Ballerinas Don't Wear Glasses*—Ainslie Manson and Dean Griffiths
- *Darby: The Special Order Pup*—Alexandra Day
- *Dog Breath*—Dav Pilkey
- *Little White Dogs Can't Jump*—Bruce Whatley
- *Lizzy and Skunk*—Marie-Louise Fitzpatrick
- *Porcupining*—Lisa Wheeler
- *Thunder Cake*—Patricia Polacco
- *The Wednesday Surprise*—Eve Bunting

Question-answer stories:

- *Good-bye Geese*—Nancy White Carlstrom
- *Who Hops?*—Katie Davis
- *Winter Lullaby*—Barbara Seuling
- *Why?*—Lila Prap

Repeating-phrase stories:

- *Harriet, You'll Drive Me Wild*—Mem Fox
- *Have You Ever Done That?*—Julie Larios
- *The Important Book*—Margaret Wise Brown
- *Koala Lou*—Mem Fox
- *Mothers Are Like That*—Carol Carrick
- *Puddles*—Jonathan London
- *Turtle, Turtle, Watch Out!*—April Pulley Sayre
- *We Are Bears*—Molly Grooms and Lucia Guarnotta
- *When I Was Young in the Mountains*—Cynthia Rylant

follow a similar text pattern. However, students won't have this vocabulary. Instead, we hear such comments as, "They kind of have the same pattern." Or, "It's like the authors used the same plan." We record their thoughts and move to independent writing time. The next day, we meet them with a different stack of books and repeat the inquiry.

After three or four days of this, it's time to "officially" define text structure. We ask our students what they think of our last couple of lessons. Typically, we hear something like, "Books can follow certain patterns and there are all different kinds of patterns." And finally we step in to clear things up.

Patterns . . . that's a great way to put it. But, it's a little bit more than just a pattern. What we've been seeing here is something that writers call text structure. Text structure is like a plan or a model that writers can follow. So far we've seen that stories can go back and forth from one thing to another, or stories can go question, answer, question, answer. Some stories don't repeat anything; they seem to follow a similar plan. Most stories have a structure, a way to organize all the things that are happening.

The next step is to create a resource. Our chart usually begins something like this, "Authors must choose a text structure to help them organize their thoughts . . ." We then make a two-column list—text structure and texts we see this in. We begin by adding the lists of books that we've shared with them over the last couple of days. As the days go on, we share a few more books with interesting text structures that we feel might be useful to our writers. Of course, the chart stays up, and as we read more and more, we are bound to stumble upon new and different structures to add.

The list of possible text structures could go on and on. (Again, Ray's *Wondrous Words* is a fabulous resource.) However, as we have worked with students and revised our teaching of text structures, we have found that some structures lend themselves more easily to our students' writing. We use the following list as a starting place. From there, the list grows a bit differently each year and with different grade levels. A few of these possible student-friendly text structures include:

- **Linear story**—problem, events, solution

- **Circle story**—home-away-home, the story ends just where it began

- **Frame story or story within a story**—one story takes place within another story

- **Cause-effect story**—one event leads directly to another event like a chain reaction

- **Back-and-forth story**—often a dialogue between two narrators or a relationship between opposing points of view

- **Letter texts**—story is told through an exchange of letters or as a series of letters from one character written over time

- **Cumulative texts**—using repetition, each page adds layers to the story

- **Repeating-phrase texts**—story is maintained through the use of an important repeating line

- **Question-answer text**—story may ask a central question and attempt to answer it or it may consist of a series of questions and answers

Most of what we now know and understand about text structure we learned alongside our students. In the beginning, we went in with a few vague ideas and discovered more possible structures than we ever knew existed. We were learning how to view writing in a different way. At this point, we would have no idea how to teach writing without a great deal of emphasis on text structure. A close study of this topic affords our students a plan, a map, a possible route to take as they begin to tell their stories. Introducing text structure has proved to be a missing link in trying to get our students to write something a bit more interesting. Knowing how to use a text structure is very empowering to our young writers. Likewise, the use of text structure makes reading their work much more enjoyable for their audience.

The Role of Revision

Another important component of the writing process that is truly audience-driven is the idea of rereading what's already been written. We need to teach all students to look again at their writing so that they can fix up any errors and make changes in order to make the writing stronger.

We do not believe that revision is merely one step in the writing process. We do not believe that writers revise only after a piece is written. Instead, writers continuously revise—they are always on the lookout for ways to improve the writing. We teach revision—looking again—by modeling, modeling, and more modeling. It's difficult to look at our mentor authors' finished, published pieces and discuss how it was revised. (Although we do make great use of what authors have to say about the revision process.) We need to show our students how to stop, look back, think about what is on the page, and then act on the analysis.

Again, we need to bring our students' writing to the forefront. We are always on the lookout for their revision, whether intentional or not. We look for an editing correction or a rewriting based on new craft knowledge.

We bring this writer before the class and ask him to explain what he had first and what he changed it to. We then lead the class to see how the change made the writing stronger and more interesting to the audience.

A word of caution concerning young writers and the revision process: In our writing classrooms, revision doesn't always make the writing better. Especially with the youngest students, revision may actually make the writing even less perfect than it started out to be! Sometimes students take out way too much or try to include so many more details that the writing becomes cumbersome. We typically think of revision as making writing better and stronger. It's difficult for the perfectionist teacher within us to accept the revised yet lesser piece of writing. It took some time, but we've learned to realize that revision is just another one of those writing tools that must be played with and used often in order for the writer to have full control of it. So even if the revision process backfires once in a while, it's more advantageous to support the continual use (and occasional misuse) of the process than to scare our young writers away from trying to revise at all.

Learning to Revise From Authors

Any one of the following quotations makes a great mini-lesson focus while studying revision. Share the quotation and discuss together what the author means and how that can enhance the writing in the classroom.

◼ **I love revision. Where else can spilled milk be turned into ice cream?**

—Katherine Paterson

◼ **It's never perfect when I write it down the first time, or the second, or the fifth time. But it always gets better as I go over it and over it.**

—Jane Yolen

◼ **Writers don't write writing, they write reading.**

—Avi

◼ **The difference between the right word and the nearly right word is the same as that between lightning and the lightning bug.**

—Mark Twain

◼ **You can't sit down and expect something golden and beautiful and wise to spring forth from your fingers the first time you write . . . writing means rewriting.**

—Kate DiCamillo

As we learned to think about revision in such developmental ways, we also needed to take a very close look at what we were expecting students across the grade levels to do. We knew that when writers look over their work, they can both edit for spelling, grammar, and punctuation and they can rewrite for the sound of the writing. However, can we expect all of our writers to do this? We found that just because we ask all of our writers across grade levels to revise, that doesn't mean all students are revising in the same ways. Take a look at the following chart, which sets up a sequence for how we can nurture and develop the revising strategy.

Grade Level (or comparable ability level)	What Revision Looks Like
1	▪ Rereading to be sure the writing says just what you want it to (Help is often needed to actually make the changes, but the writer knows something is amiss.) ▪ Adding on a few words or details to the writing or illustration to tell a bit more ▪ Adding labels to pictures ▪ Checking to be sure the picture matches the print ▪ Checking to be sure the audience can "read" it—neatness, sound spelling, appropriate letter size ▪ Attempting to include a recently discovered writer's craft ▪ Eventually checking for spaces, appropriate capitals, and periods
2/3	▪ All of the above ▪ Thinking again about the topic and trying to include a new idea ▪ Attempting to include a stronger lead or ending ▪ Beginning to see how some ideas do not really fit into the piece ▪ Changing some verbs to stronger action words ▪ Adding specific details to create a more vivid picture in the reader's mind ▪ Checking for correct punctuation use (. ? ! , ' . . .) ▪ Checking to be sure there is a clear beginning, middle, and end
4/5	▪ All of the above ▪ Checking for correct punctuation use (" " : ; —) ▪ Thinking again about the topic and rewriting using a different text structure ▪ Rewriting entire sections and/or removing unimportant parts ▪ Changing words for specificity ▪ Checking for variety among sentence patterns ▪ Checking for subject-verb agreement ▪ Checking to see if the point of view is consistent ▪ Reviewing research again and changing or adding new information

One thing that jumps out when you review this chart is the fact that we are including things not necessarily referred to as a revision. Many of the revisions we see our students make are actually editing or proofreading changes. We know this. Our students also know that editing means checking over their work for awkward sentences or simple word-choice errors. They know that when they are looking for misspellings or punctuation, they are actually proofreading. We've used these terms and we've talked about them when they come up as we learn about various authors.

But what we now know is that if we ask students to continually reread their writing, first revising in broad strokes, then for some editing, and finally for proofreading, we are going to lose their interest pretty quickly. We also know from our own writing that this small-step, sequential approach to writing is not realistic. Our revision process is much more recursive. We constantly reread and make small changes. Often we know that we must go back and make large changes. All of these steps are important to the development of strong writing. However, it is not necessary to do them one at a time. By making the "rules" simpler, we get more students to buy in to the process and more students to achieve success with revision.

In our classrooms, then, we no longer find the need for elaborate bulletin boards that announce where each student is working in the five-step writing process. As we learn to teach writing in a more natural way, we see that by asking students to follow the same lockstep process each time, we relegate writing to yet another activity to be done a certain, teacher-directed way. There is very little personal responsibility or power in such a system. Instead we focus on the fact that good writers must read and reread their work. They must make changes so that their work can become stronger. They must do all they can and use all they know to ensure an easy and fascinating read for their audience.

"Teacher to Teacher"

Another way we teach the importance and ever-presence of revision is by reminding students to begin each independent writing time by rereading what they wrote last time. Students are discouraged from picking up their pencil right away. We train them to read first, remember where they were, and get their thoughts together before diving in. It's a great revising success when a student comes to us at the end of writing to say they didn't have time to do anything new; they spent the time making yesterday's writing better.

CHAPTER 8

Studying the Craft of Writing

 FOURTH-GRADE CLASS GATHERS TOGETHER, READY TO PARTICIPATE IN A MINI-LESSON ON TEXT STRUCTURE AS BARBARA TELLS THEM TO USE THEIR WRITERS' EYES AND EARS. She has been teaching a series of lessons on text structure to assist them in organizing their stories and developing stronger endings. As Barbara reads *Homerun* by Robert Burleigh and discusses the circular structure of the book, it soon becomes obvious that these students read like writers. Throughout the lesson, hands pop up. The students are eager to talk about what they notice:

- the lead sentence of only four words
- the bubble gum cards on every other page
- the fragmented sentences
- the sepia-toned pictures
- the close-up illustrations of people
- the invented hyphenated words ("nothing-quite-like-it," "boy-fire," "calling-out")
- and even the dedication at the end of the book to the author's father "—who loved the game."

These students know what goes into writing books because they are writers.

From the first day of school, we immerse our students in literature. Our students participate in Reading Workshop and have time for independent reading. They are read to throughout the day, and their classroom libraries are rich with literature. There is a host of resource books and materials available for writing and writing ideas; and if that's not enough, students have access to the school's media center to research topics on which they are writing.

We have structured our environment in this way because we believe that in order for students to write well they need to read widely and to be read to regularly. We know that this is necessary at all grades, not just in the beginning years. During our Reading Workshop mini-lessons, we spend a great deal of time helping students develop a sense of story and an understanding of the elements of literature. As they learn about plot development, they identify the problem, solution, and changes that occur in the story. As they identify the characters, they become aware of how the characters change and develop. And as the students identify the setting's time and place, they notice how the author indicates the passage of time. These understandings are built through strong daily instruction and discussion. However, we know this is not enough if we want our students to be good writers. It's not enough to simply identify these characteristics. We want our writers to apply them in their own work.

Through reading to children and exposing them to good literature, we help them appreciate the techniques writers use and the decisions that authors make to craft their work. We do this as we point out the story's structure, varied text formats, and interesting word choices. Every time we read aloud we teach writing.

Looking Closely at the "How" of Writing

When our students read, we tell them to read with their "reader's eyes" and to pay attention to the words and message of the writer. But when we want them to look at how a book was written, we tell them to use their "writer's eyes." When we do this, we read the book differently. We look at the techniques the author used to craft the book and think about the decisions that went into the writing.

For example, one of the things writers do is consider how to structure their book. Is it a linear or circular format? Is there a back-and-forth format, or is it a question and answer approach? Is it poetic or lyrical in nature? Has the text been addressed in a journal or letter format? Just when you think you have addressed a number of possibilities, a student may bring a book to you and ask, "What structure did this writer use?" After taking a look, you realize there is a story within a story—still another text structure. Your students are now reading with their writer's eyes. They are now looking at writing craft.

Crafting techniques include much more than text structure. Writers' decisions involve carefully choosing words. Some writers seem to know just the right way to combine words. Think about the times you pick up a novel and are transported to a place because of the way the author establishes the setting. You feel the humidity as you wind through the gardens of Charleston. You see the blackness of the night as you gaze up from the porch of an abandoned cabin. You even smell the sweat of the horses as they return to the barn. We find ourselves lost in books because of the language and find ourselves thinking, "What can I do to express myself like that?" But we also need to ask ourselves, "What can I do to help my students notice the language in books to improve their choice of words in their own writing?"

While Barbara was reading *My Mama Had a Dancing Heart* to a group of students, Angel asked her why she had a pink sticky note on a page. She responded that she just loved the words on that page. "Listen," she said. "Let me read that page again." During the independent reading time, Barbara noticed that Keyana had cut a narrow strip of paper out and with Scotch tape attached it to a page in the book she was creating. When Barbara asked what she was doing, Keyana said, "I'm marking this page in my book just like you did." Wow! And if that wasn't enough, Keyana showed Barbara how she was revising her writing to have a sing-song rhythm to it since she also liked the sounds of the words in *My Mama Had a Dancing Heart.*

Our students notice the techniques that authors use to create books, and they try them in their own writing. As we examine the books they write, we gain a true appreciation of all that they have learned about writing and constructing books. In examining some second-grade books, we see evidence that students know that:

- books have covers and title pages
- books have dedication pages
- pictures in a book match the text
- the text can be at the top or the bottom of pages
- some pages only have one sentence
- some pages only have pictures
- some pictures spread across two pages
- some text spreads across two pages
- books can be written from different points of view
- ellipsis can be used to continue the text on the next page
- the font can be changed for effective purposes
- books need a beginning and an ending
- books can be revised to make them sound better
- poetry books look different than story books
- nonfiction books use real photos and picture captions
- nonfiction books contain facts on topics
- some books include facts at the end of the book
- books can contain a table of contents, an index, and/or a glossary
- books have information on the backs of them to make you want to read them
- books include information about the author

We are using our Writer's Eyes. We notice...

there's a repeating phrase
he uses lots of ands
he's changing the setting quickly
long ands
   (climbed and climed and climbed)

there are clues in the pictures
lots of little pics to show lots of things
give something its own
   page it becomes special

▲ As students notice the craft in writing, we quickly chart our ideas to help us remember. (Even teachers misspell words when writing on the fly!)

We've not directly taught any of them. We've made careful book selections, brought them to our writers, and asked them to share what they notice. It is this constant returning to texts for conversation that builds a strong foundation for the student writers.

"Teacher to Teacher"

Whenever possible, we bring books that we've already read together to our writers' meetings. It is most important to read, enjoy, and understand a book first with "reader's eyes." After students know what the book is about, then they can begin to pull it apart into crafting components. It is really asking too much for them to understand the story AND deconstruct the author's work at the same time. Before diving in with, "What do you notice?" we go through the book and together we remind each other of what the book was about.

Bradley's book on earning money includes a dedication—to the mints (not be confused with candy mints). ▶

Byeing a Hamster

Contends
Geeting a hamster
What you need
Food & water
bhelter
A good owner

◀ *A page from Ellie's book shows she knows about a table of contents and includes one in her book about buying a hamster.*

dedicated to all of the mints.

mint

Craft Ideas That Matter to Student Writers

Word choice:

- Adding sound words
- Making up new words
- Using "joining-in" words
  (choosing repetitive words to encourage choral reading)
- Rollercoaster "ands"
  (using *ands* for repetition,
  e.g., ran and ran and ran)
- Using that "just right" word
- Choosing words to fit the tone or mood

Text structure:

- ABC
- Counting
- Circle
- Back-and-forth
- Question-answer
- Repeating-phrase
- Story within a story
- Journal or diary
- Letter
- Ending with a question
- Ending with a change

Text format:

- Wavy words across the page
- Bold words
- Big and small words
- Two-page spread "picture page"
- Pictures that "grow" (fold-out pages)
- Turning the book an unusual way
- Word color
- Text written in a shape to match the idea, topic, or concept

Other:

- Ellipses
- Using parentheses to explain or clarify
- Adding About the Author pages
- Writing clues on the back cover
- Leaving picture clues for the reader
- Adding speech bubbles to illustrations
- Making pop-up or lift-the-flap books
- Explanatory text at the bottom of the page

Authors as Mentors

Using a mentor author means taking a look at the author's craft and possibly using some of those ideas in our own writing. It means thinking of possible decisions the author made to construct the text.

If we look at Bill Martin's book *Brown Bear, Brown Bear*, we notice that the book has repetition and that the repetition leads to the next page in the book. We may speculate that the text was written to help young children make predictions, to learn colors, and to feel comfortable in joining in and repeating a refrain. Many young writers write stories like *Brown Bear* and add their own colors and characters. However, Tyler went beyond noticing the animals and the colors and noticed the ending to the book. Bill Martin does not end *Brown Bear* with one more animal but with the teacher looking at the children. Tyler liked this surprise ending and used a surprise ending in his own patterned story. Tyler is now using Bill Martin as a mentor author to help him structure his story with a surprise ending.

In order to be successful, the writing style and level must be appropriate to the level of the students. The students must see learning from a mentor author as doable. The text must match what the child is capable of constructing.

Writers Who Make Strong Mentor Authors in the Classroom

For primary classrooms:

- Eric Carle
- Donald Crews
- Joy Cowley
- Lois Ehlert
- Mem Fox
- Kevin Henkes
- Ezra Jack Keats
- Bill Martin, Jr.
- Robert Munsch
- Cynthia Rylant
- David Shannon
- Audrey and Don Wood

For intermediate grades:

- Eve Bunting
- Sharon Creech
- Kevin Henkes
- Karen Hesse
- Patricia MacLachlan
- Patricia Polacco
- Gary Paulsen
- Cynthia Rylant
- Jerry Spinelli
- Jane Yolen
- Charlotte Zolotow

Many authors write in ways that are helpful to young authors of all ages. Kevin Henkes and Cynthia Rylant are good examples. Although their texts tend to be longer, even young students exposed to much literature will notice their writing styles and the way the story is structured. A third grader noticed that Kevin Henkes "always writes in threes. He repeats himself. I can write like Kevin Henkes." And his next story about sailing reflected his mentor author.

It is obvious that Forrest (above) knows sailing, but he also knows author's craft. Forrest is not writing about the same things as Kevin Henkes or using his characters or story ideas. Rather he has structured his writing in a similar way.

Ariel (at right) also used mentor authors as she borrowed a technique for her writing. She noticed the effectiveness of a repeated phrase in the books *When I Was Young in the Mountains* (Rylant) and *Harriet You'll Drive Me Wild* (Fox). She crafted the following piece with a repeating phrase that works.

With our continued guidance, students learn to pay attention to carefully chosen and descriptive words. Our students know we have some favorite books that they hear over and over again.

⁂ They appreciate the language as we read about the moose in *Up North at the Cabin* (Chall) as "he shakes his great head, rocking branches of bone as he bellows a warning."

> "He loves the way the halyard's clank on the silver mast, and the way his feet slide on the slippery deck. He loves the way her white sails luft in the breeze. And he loves the way she heels over in a strong wind."
>
> —By Forrest V.

For early readers we have used books they've become familiar with in guided reading. These books are very patterned and predictable, and students find success writing books with a similar, simple format. "I can ride my bike. I can tie my shoes. I can climb a tree. I can read my books." Even more simply written is a book on hearts. "Pink hearts. Red hearts. Striped hearts. I like hearts."

> Once there was a boy named Darcy that had a project due Friday, but it just happened to be Monday. He was not worried at all. "I have plenty of time," he said to himself.
>
> So Tuesday passed. His friend Ariel got a poster board for her project, but Darcy was swinging on a swing thinking to himself, "I have plenty of time."
>
> Wednesday was here. Ariel got modeling clay for her project. What did Darcy do? He played video games while he could be doing his project, but NO he has "plenty" of time.
>
> Thursday came and Ariel got a cardboard stage for her project. Still, Darcy was playing tag with other kids. Thinking to himself "I have plenty of time, I have a whole night . . . Wait, just one night? Oh no! I'm going to be in so much trouble!"
>
> So he went to school that day in fear of a big FAT F-. He went to his friend Ariel for advice but all she said was, "You should have worked on it when you had plenty of time . . ."
>
> —By Ariel G.

Once students begin to notice the craft of some authors, you will see it appearing in their own writing. They may try their hand at writing with fragments, or creating their own words, structuring their writing differently. However, we advise our fifth-grade students about the type of writing that is expected of them on the state writing tests. In preparation for these tests, we do a genre unit on writing for the state tests.

* They cheer on *Billywise* (Nicholls) as the young owl learns to fly: "he longed to swoop, loop-the-loop, to slide through the air, as silently as moonlight to glide through the midnight air."

* They relive toasting marshmallows as we read *Camping* (Hundal) and see "the black charry bits scabbed to stick, stuck to fingers. Burnt."

* They notice how Mary Lyn Ray creates some of her own words to get the right feeling and images in her book *Red Rubber Boot Day*. In noticing " . . . window-splashy rain" and the "Red rubber made-for-rain boots," the students talk about creating their own words in their writing.

Look at all these great teaching points. As we talk about what authors do and consider the choices they make, we show students *how to write*. We pull out some writing we are currently working on and demonstrate how we apply similar techniques to our writing. This modeling helps bridge the gap between the craft discussions and the actual writing.

Selecting appropriate authors and texts is crucial. Often, we have to rely on instincts. We know our students. We know their interests. And we know their writing. Through exposure to good literature and techniques that authors use, our students will, with our encouragement, recognize these devices and try them in their own writing. After a while, it becomes hard to tell just who is the mentor author. As one of our little ones said, "David Shannon writes just like me."

Using Texts to Support Student Topics

The majority of our students don't seem to have trouble coming up with topics for their writing. In the primary grades, it seems to help that they are writing books, and they have so many things they are interested in. One day Justin may be writing a book about his baby brother. Another day he is writing a chapter book about school. And the following week he is trying his hand at a book about poisonous snakes. If students have difficulty coming up with topics, we help them think about what they are really curious about.

In the intermediate grades, students tend to write what they know a lot about and are passionate about. We tend to do the same thing. Barbara has no trouble coming up with stories about her cat while Marybeth has an endless supply of stories about her daughter. By sharing these examples with our students, they see there are some topics they really know a lot about. Our role is to help the students come up with their own ideas and to provide them with some mentor authors to help craft their work. These young writers need us to remind them of how authors can help them structure their story and/or improve their choice of words.

▲ *Edan knows a lot about his friend—his topic for this book. He crafted his book after he was inspired by the format in* Cookie's Week *by Cindy Ward.*

Suggested Literature for Leads

We are always looking for great leads to show students how writers hook their readers. Our list includes just a sampling of some good leads.

The story begins by establishing the setting:

- *The Bat Boy and His Violin*—Gavin Curtis
- *Circle of Gold*—Candy Dawson Boyd (chapter book)
- *Lola*—Loufane
- *Poppy*—Avi (chapter book)
- *A Secret Place*—Eve Bunting
- *Up North at the Cabin*—Marsha Wilson Chall

A question hooks the reader:

- *Charlotte's Web*—E. B. White (chapter book)
- *Duke Ellington*—Andrea Davis Pinkney
- *Momma, Where Are You From?*—Marie Bradby

Dialogue often begins a book:

- *The Comeback Dog*—Jane Resh Thomas (chapter book)
- *Emily's Art*—Peter Catalanotto
- *Number the Stars*—Lois Lowry (chapter book)
- *The Raft*—Jim LaMarche
- *The Story of the Sea Glass*—Anne Wescott Dodd
- *The Train to Somewhere*—Eve Bunting

Some leads get the reader in the action immediately:

- *Harriet*—Deborah Inkpen
- *Knuffle Bunny*—Mo Willems
- *Snow Treasure*—Marie McSwigan (chapter book)
- *A Story for Bear*—Dennis Haseley

Surprising facts are often used to catch the reader's attention:

- *A. Lincoln and Me*—Louise Borden
- *The Cats in Krasinski Square*—Karen Hesse
- *Eleanor*—Barbara Cooney
- *Fireboat*—Maira Kalman
- *The Other Dog*—Madeleine L'Engle
- *Wilma Unlimited*—Kathleen Krull

Suggested Literature for Endings

O ur students know their stories should not end with simply "THE END." To help them finish their stories, we rely on some mentor authors. The books don't necessarily focus on the last sentence but on the structure of ending stories.

The ending surprises the reader:

- *Charlie Anderson*—Barbara Abercrombie
- *Darby: The Special-Order Pup*—Alexandra Day
- *Dory Story*—Jerry Pallotta
- *First Day Jitters*—Julie Danneberg
- *Wednesday Surprise*—Eve Bunting

Some endings leave you "feeling good":

- *Amber on the Mountain*—Tony Johnston
- *Fireflies*—Julie Brinckloe
- *Silver Packages*—Cynthia Rylant
- *The Whales*—Cynthia Rylant
- *Wilfrid Gordon MacDonald Partridge*—Mem Fox

Some books end with a message or moral:

- *Koala Lou*—Mem Fox
- *Lilly's Purple Plastic Purse*—Kevin Henkes
- *Seven Blind Mice*—Steven Young
- *Stellaluna*—Janell Cannon

Endings are sometimes ambiguous and leave you wondering:

- *Fly Away Home*—Eve Bunting
- *Grandpa and Bo*—Kevin Henkes
- *Hey, Little Ant*—Phillip and Hannah Hoose
- *Miss Rumphius*—Barbara Cooney

Many stories end in a circular format so they end pretty much where they started:

- *The Great Gracie Chase*—Cynthia Rylant
- *My Mama Had a Dancing Heart*—Libba Moore Gray
- *One Dark Night*—Hazel Hutchins
- *The Paperboy*—Dav Pilkey
- *The Relatives Came*—Cynthia Rylant
- *The Sick Day*—Patricia MacLachlan

Sample Author's Craft Mini-lessons

Using a Mentor Author to Enhance a Story

In this mini-lesson with a group of fourth graders, Barbara discusses one of the stories she has been working on. Her goal is to get the students to recognize how a technique used by a mentor author can help strengthen her own writing.

TEACHER: *I was thinking about the story I wrote about my grandmother—the one about making a lemon meringue pie. I really like the story, but I was wondering if I should include some background information about my grandmother.*

STUDENT: You mean because she was deaf?

T: *Yes, because I think it's important for the reader to know how special my grandmother was.*

S: And because it was long time ago.

T: *Yes, it was a long time ago, and her deafness was more of a problem then. So I was thinking I would use one of my favorite mentor authors to help me. I went through some of my books by Patricia Polacco because I know she often provides some background information in the beginning or at the end of her books. I thought I might want to try that.*

S: Oh, you could tell the reader about your grandma before they read your story about making the pie together.

Many of our charts stay up a long time, and we continuously add to them as we learn of new techniques.

T: *That's what I'm thinking of. Let's take a look at some of Patricia Polacco's books.*

(Barbara shares the following titles: *Thunder Cake, My Ol' Man, Dear Mr. Falker, Mrs. Mack, Betty Doll,* and a special student version of *My Rotten Redheaded Older Brother.*)

I'm going to try writing some background information about my grandmother, and then I'll decide if I'm going to include it at the beginning of my story or at the end.

S: If you do it at the end, it might kind of surprise the reader.

T: *I like that idea. I was thinking of that too. This way, the reader could think everything is absolutely normal with the grandmother and*

We notice Author's Craft when we read with our writer's eyes.
We can craft our writing.
We can...
· Use a repeating phrase
· Change the setting
· Make a long time with ...and...and...and
· Use sound effect words
· Change the shape of words
· Switch-a-roo ending

*granddaughter baking together, and then after the story the reader would learn
what makes it so special. I think I'll try it both ways and let you help me decide
tomorrow which way you think is better.*

*Today as you write, think about how an author can help you. Does your story
need some background information that you could add at the beginning or end?
When you go to your seats and read your story, decide if the extra information
would improve your story. OK, it's time for you to get to work. Off you go.*

Later, during conferencing, Barbara makes note of students who try such a writing
technique with their memoirs. At share time, she asks Robert to share how he
incorporated this technique with his memoir.

Noticing Craft Techniques in a Picture Book

TEACHER: *Writers, yesterday at reading time we read Kevin Henkes' new book,* Kitten's First
Full Moon. *And we read it to really understand the story. We went slowly and we
thought about things as we read. I ended my journal with a question, why were
the illustrations in black and white? His other books were not done that way.
Then I thought, we've read so many other Henkes books, but we've never gone
back to his books with our writers' eyes. So, today I thought, since we already
know the story, we could ask Mr. Henkes some questions. I wondered if we could
learn any craft tips from this book or any of his other books. Maybe we could use
some craft techniques that Mr. Henkes uses in
our own books. Are you ready to revisit the
book, this time with our writers' eyes?*

STUDENT: Yes

T: *Let's first go through the story and remember
what was happening—so we won't be
distracted by what the book was about.*

(Marybeth goes through a picture walk with
students and together they retell the story.)

S: Maybe the black and white is because it was
nighttime.

T: *We talked about that yesterday. The whole story
takes place in one night. Maybe the colors were
picked to show nighttime. Would you agree that
that was a crafting decision by the author?*

S: Yes.

T: *Well then, let's start a helping chart for
ourselves. Let's write, "Hey, Mr. Henkes, what
craft can we learn from you?" We'll add that he*

Hey, Mr. Henkes! What craft
can we learn from you?
· B. and W. pictures
· strong words
· humor
· repeating phrase page is
  different from other pages
· show something happen
  for a long time →
  same word over

chose black-and-white illustrations. Now let's take another look. Remember, we're not talking about what happened in the story, we're talking about how the author crafted the book.

(Marybeth returns to the book and begins to slowly reread parts of it.)

"She closed her eyes and stretched her neck and opened her mouth and licked . . ." What do you notice here? Any decisions Kevin Henkes made on this page?

S: He's trying to tell us that she's trying to get to the moon.

T: Yes, I think what you're trying to say is that the author didn't just say, "The kitten is trying to get to the moon." Did he?

S: No.

T: No, he really stretched it out. "She closed her eyes and stretched her neck and opened her mouth and licked . . ." He's really putting a picture in our minds. One of his craft decisions is to use strong, interesting words (notes this on the chart). Now, what else do you notice about this part, "But Kitten only ended up with a bug on her tongue"?

S: That's a little bit ridiculous.

T: Yes, and we talked about something like that before when we read Froggy Eats Out.

(Marybeth pulls out the book to serve as a visual reminder.)

The author had a message for us, but he also used humor. He made the book funny. Authors use humor—something funny— to make their book interesting. Using humor is crafting (notes this on chart). Has anyone here used humor in your books?

S: I made the ending of my penguin book funny when they all jumped in the water.

S: I tried to put funny faces on the flowers in my illustrations so they'd be more interesting.

T: That's exactly what we are talking about; using humor is crafting. OK, let's keep going. What else can we learn? "Still there was the little bowl of milk just waiting." Anything, writers?

S: The author is using a repeating phrase.

T: Oh, does anyone else see this?

S: Yes.

(As Marybeth jumps ahead and shares this phrase that repeats throughout the whole book, the students join in as she reads.)

S: Hey, on the repeating-phrase pages, the words go across two pages and they're both white pages. On the other pages it is black and white.

T: *Hmm, Did anyone else notice this? Why might he have done this?*

S: It makes it pop out a little more.

T: *I'm not sure anyone of us has ever crafted a book that way. Have any authors in here set up a page like that? Usually, we make a plan to put words that go together on only one side of the page.*

S: I did that in my snake book.

T: *You did? Tell us about that.*

S: It was my fact book about snakes and on two pages across, I wrote, "Did you know that snakes have venom?"

T: *Was that sentence different from other sentences in the book? Is that why you chose to make the words on two pages?*

S: Really, I thought the venom was the cool part, so I wanted it to have two pages.

T: *So you crafted your page in a way that you were able to make this sentence really stick out and seem important? That's great! All right, now how can we write all this up on our helping chart?*

S: The repeating-phrase page is different from other pages.

       (Marybeth charts the response.)

T: *Wait a second, I'm thinking . . . have we ever read a book where the repeating phrase gets its own page?*

S: I think that's a new one!

T: *So, writers, that's another decision you can make. Do you put the phrase right after the other words, or do you give it its own page? I think we have time to find one more crafting idea in this book.*

       (Marybeth continues reading.)

       "So she ran to the tallest tree she could find and she climbed and climbed and climbed to the very top." What do you notice?

S: There's a repeating phrase, climbed and climbed and climbed.

T: *I see what you are saying, but I wouldn't call that a repeating phrase. I'd say that he is saying the same word over and over again. Hey, that reminds me again of that Froggy book* (pulls out the book and reads): *"After the waiter came and took their orders, they waited and waited and waited." Hmmm, did it take a really long time for their food to get there?*

S: Yes!

T:	*Did Kitten climb for a really long time?*
S:	Yes!
S:	Oohhh, they're both saying something took a really long time!
T:	*And how are they able to show us this?*
S:	By using those ands and the same word over and over.
T:	*What if I want to say I ran a long time?*
S:	You could say, "I ran and I ran and I ran."
T:	*Absolutely, so let's add to our chart. "Show something happened for a long time by using the same word over and over." We can definitely use that in our books.*
	All right, wow, we didn't even go through the whole book but Mr. Henkes has taught us to think about black-and-white pictures, using strong words, using humor, giving repeating phrases their own page, and making things happen for a long time using and.
	Now, let's see writers. Melissa, tell us what your book is about.
S:	Lots and lots of clothes.
T:	*Ah, yes, the clothes. Is there anything on our chart that will help you revise today? Is there some craft idea you've learned that will make your work stronger today?*
S:	I think I need to put a better picture in my audience's head, like when he said . . . "She closed her eyes and stretched her neck and open her mouth and licked . . ."
T:	*Does anyone else have an idea for revising now?*
S:	I might change the part where my family goes in an airplane to say, "We flew and flew and flew."
T:	*That will really help us know, in an interesting way, that you were flying for a long time!*
	OK, this is what we'll share today . . . if you've done something today to revise your writing using a craft idea from Kevin Henkes.
S:	And, that will be a nice way to end today.
T:	*Sure would. All right writers, let's get started. We need to go and craft our work so that our audience enjoys the story.*

This lesson took place toward the end of the year in a first-grade classroom. However, it could easily have happened in any grade level. Marybeth did not come knowing exactly what she would end up with on the chart. She had a few ideas of what craft techniques were employed. Admittedly, she read certain parts in such a way that she knew the students would "discover" the craft on their own.

The connections to other books were not planned in advance. Those connections truly came off the top of her head. These connections are crucial if we want our students to believe that the craft of writing is a true, real-world idea. We're not just making it up! We don't need to know everything about every book we read. However, the more we teach this way, the more examples we have in our minds about how books are related. And often, it's the students who remind us of where we've seen the technique before.

It's also important to notice how Marybeth willingly accepted the thoughts of her students. In an attempt to clear things up for others and to begin to create a common language within the classroom, she often restated the student comment. We use phrases such as, "OK, so what you are saying is . . ." We want students to know that we will use their ideas but the student comment is often verbose or clunky. We want all students to be able to take the key information away from the lesson, and we want all students to be able to remember this information at a later date. We make sure to repeat ourselves over and over. We try to "spin" the student's comment to fit in with our agreed-upon common language about writing. We need to make the connections clear.

Narrowing the Topic

When students write and write and write, their pieces often end up too long and boring. Or sometimes we just get a listing of events or descriptions. We try to show students how to narrow their topic and write about a specific occurrence. This is what Barbara had in mind as she led third graders through this mini-lesson.

TEACHER: *I just found a great book that I want to share with you today. I chose it because some of you have been writing stories that are going on and on and on, and you're not sure how much to tell and when to stop. This book is called* Roller Coaster *by Marla Frazee. As I read it I want you to notice how the author focuses on just one roller coaster ride, not the whole visit to the amusement park. Sometimes some of you try to write about your day at Busch Gardens, and you end up writing about everyone you go with, everyone you see, everything you eat, and everything you do. And even though you remember your trip to Busch Gardens as wonderful, you aren't pleased with your story about it. Let's see if this book will help you focus on just one part of your trip.*

(Barbara reads the book to the students, stopping occasionally to point out the illustrations of people waiting in line for the ride, to focus on the short amount of time that is passing in the book, and to call attention to how the author moves the story along.)

STUDENT: I think it's funny that the man got scared of the ride and got out of line.

T: *Wasn't it neat that you could tell that from the illustrations but it wasn't mentioned in the story?*

S: At first I thought it was the little girl who was scared.

T: *But you noticed the clues to help you figure it out.*

S: You were right when you said the author didn't write about the whole trip to the amusement park. It was just waiting in line for the roller coaster and then the fun on the ride.

T: *And it made for a great story. The author just focused on a specific time—just the roller coaster ride. I bet you can try that with your writing. Instead of writing about your entire camping trip, you could write about toasting marshmallows one evening with your family. Or rather than writing about your birthday party and all the things you received, you could write about helping your dad put your new bike together. Good writers try to tell about one special time. I bet you could try that.*

S: I could write about the night we had to race Mom to the hospital because my brother was being born.

T: *That could be an exciting night to write about. Or, maybe you could make it smaller and simply write about the crazy drive to the hospital.*

S: Instead of telling you everything about my dog, I could tell you about the day we were scared he was lost and how we found him.

T: *I bet that would be a great story with a happy ending. It sounds like you are getting the idea now.*

During conference time, Barbara provides direction for those needing to focus their stories and narrow their topics. While some students independently grasp the idea, others need additional support. At share time, students are asked to simply share how they are revising their stories to narrow the focus. For example, instead of reading their revised story, they can simply say, "Instead of writing about my summer vacation, I'm just writing about my first plane trip." It's not always necessary for them to share their entire rewritten pieces. However, if some students have had some immediate success and it's a major breakthrough, then by all means give them the stage.

CHAPTER 9

Studying Different Types of Writing

 RICH LITERARY EXPERIENCES EXPOSE STUDENTS TO A VARIETY OF GENRES. IDEALLY, THESE EXPERIENCES SHOULD TAKE READERS BEYOND THE TEXT, FILLING THEIR HEADS AND HEARTS WITH LITERATURE. With strong instruction, the print comes to life as students become a part of the story, as they hear the voices of the characters and experience the events. Students recognize well-crafted writing and appreciate the importance of word choice—of finding those just-right words. They appreciate the structure of nonfiction as they gain knowledge through reading informative texts and as they share their knowledge in writing such texts. Throughout their study of various genres, students develop their own rich language and vocabulary, strengthening their own writing as they go.

Genre Experiences

Our school district's curriculum spells out for each grade level what genres our students should be exposed to and what written products they should be able to produce. While students may be able to read and have knowledge of most literary genres, they may not be able to create their own. First graders are exposed to fantasy and fairy tales, but they would certainly not be expected to create their own. While fifth graders may enjoy science fiction, it is not an easy genre for students to write. We'll offer suggestions for possible genre writing and share what our students have had success writing at various levels.

Through our Reading and Writing Workshops, we expose our students to rich literature. Our first-grade students hear the language of fantasies, folk and fairy tales, realistic fiction, nonfiction, and poetry. By second and third grade, they are also listening to and reading biographies, autobiographies, tall tales, and mysteries. Fourth and fifth graders are adding historical fiction, humor, adventure, science fiction, and modern fantasy to their reading repertoire.

Although we recognize the importance of exposing children to various genres, we do not expect them to write all forms. Many genres are just too difficult for students to pull off well. We are very interested in setting the students up for genuine success: strong writing built on a personal idea, not merely a weak reproduction of a mystery or fairy tale. At the same time, we do want them to go beyond keeping journals and writing memoirs.

In looking over the little books written by first graders, we see pictures with captions, lists, retellings, simple stories, and nonfiction writing. Throughout the year, the books develop as the author's reading experiences develop. Their writing experiences mirror what they have been exposed to in class discussions. As students notice and talk about writing craft, it begins to appear in their own writing. Later in the year, these young writers also become very adept poets after an inquiry into the poetry genre.

Second graders continue with book writing, and we see more short stories, memoirs, and report writing. They enjoy researching topics and writing nonfiction books. This is also the year when students learn about autobiographies as they write about themselves. In second grade, it's common to see students trying their hands at poetry, especially if they are fortunate to have poetry read to them regularly.

By third grade, students have had many literary experiences and are able to try various genres. But it's an age at which many students play it safe. Some students don't take the same types of risks they did in first and second grade because they are hard at work forming paragraphs, getting the spelling correct, and writing what they know about. As a result, memoirs and report writing are common. It is our job to encourage risk-taking and the continuation of their writing passion as we help them expand their writing genre repertoire.

While fourth and fifth graders participate in Writing Workshop, much of their writing crosses curricular lines. They write biographies and keep historical journals on famous figures. In science classes, students write explanations to accompany projects, experiments, or research reports. During Writing Workshop, individuals write memoirs, short stories, nonfiction pieces, or poetry. You may see a merging of the writing and the content areas as in this poem by Ra'Quan during a study of the Civil War.

The Battlefield

By Ra'Quan J.

I am scared when I'm on the battlefield.
I hear guns going POW.
Brother watching from the window
And all he says is wow.
My mom is scared when I go out.
"I'm protecting my country," I say with a shout.
It's scary on the battlefield and now I'm dead.
Mom comes out running and screams "He's Dead."

Ra'Quan has written a number of poems over the years. One of our favorites acknowledges his passion for poetry.

A Prisoner of Poetry

By Ra'Quan J.

I'm a prisoner of poetry,
And I don't know what to do.
I find all sorts of rhyming words
Like two and shoe and boo!
I try to stop this nonsense.
It's horrible you see.
I guess I can't 'cause
I'm a prisoner of poetry.

You are probably thinking about all the genres you have exposed your students to. Some of them are a result of a very conscious plan—your district may have expectations for genre studies. What's important to note is that we can't just expose students to the various genres. We play an active part in helping them shape their genre-specific writing. If we do not, their attempts at writing in various genres will remain just that, attempts. For this reason, it is very important to consider what we can realistically expect our students to produce and produce well.

Making Genre Studies Meaningful

The purpose of the writing determines the genre the writing will take. Think about the types of reading you do and the reasons for that reading. You receive a thank-you note from friends who spent the weekend with you. You open up your favorite cookbook for a new recipe to try. You look at the directions to figure out how to install the new printer you purchased for your computer. You read several travel books as you make plans for your spring break. As you think about what you read, consider the genre. The author had a particular purpose in mind, and this purpose affected the content and form.

As we consider what our students need to know about writing in various genres, we think about how to make these writing experiences valuable and real for them. While we do this, we teach the essentials of good writing. All good writing includes descriptions, details, voice, clarity, and word choice.

The following are some examples of real writing that meet the requirements of writing in various genres while providing some real reasons to write. These experiences helped the students see that the message was as important as the form.

- After first graders went to see the Nutcracker Ballet, they wrote to thank the PTA for supporting the field trip.

- Second-grade students who received a donation of books for their classroom libraries wrote to thank the sorority for its philanthropy.

- Fifth grade students wrote to Busch Gardens because a new ride was being constructed. Since Busch Gardens is only two miles from our school, the students thought they should be the first riders because they had watched the ride's progress from their school bus as it passed every morning and every afternoon. As a result of their persuasive letter writing, they were awarded a morning at Busch Gardens to ride Apollo's Chariot before the ride was opened to the public.

- Students who were learning about informational texts developed a brochure about their classroom for parents' night.

- Fourth graders kept historical journals as they each took on the persona of a figure from history and integrated social studies knowledge with writing skills.

- Students wrote and shared biographies at a museum where the "wax figures" came to life when a spotlight was shone upon them.

- Students shared original poetry with parents and visitors in a "coffeehouse" atmosphere.

As you can see, it is easy to make genre experiences real and meaningful. By emphasizing the link between author's purpose and genre, students begin to see a need for understanding how various genres work. The more they understand the genre type, the easier it is for them to produce their own original, meaningful piece.

Genre Studies

As we have mentioned, the students' reading repertoire consists of various narrative, expository, and poetic genres. Although this background knowledge helps them in writing, they will not be required to write in all of those genres. The following chart lists genres that students are usually expected to write in successfully.

Narrative	Functional	Informational	Poetry
Personal narratives	Letters	Summaries	Rhymed
Fictional narratives	Descriptions	Learning logs	Unrhymed
Memoirs	Explanations	Reports	Patterned
Journals	Persuasive writing	Picture books	
Diaries	Procedural writing	Biography	
Picture books	Observations	Autobiography	
Short stories	Invitations	Book reviews	
Fantasy	Editorial/opinion	Literary nonfiction	
		Essay	

▲ *Consider the level of your students as you explore some of these possible writing genres.*

When deciding on expectations for writers, we keep in mind the level of our students and our school district's curriculum. And while students should not be required to write in all the genres they may be reading, they still have many writing opportunities. This writing ability grows because of strong, varied reading experiences. They know books. They know different genres. They know how to seek answers from other writers. It is our job to help them choose the appropriate genre for their message and use mentor authors as they write. We constantly strive to help students bridge the gap between what they read and what they write.

For this reason, when we teach students to write in a particular genre or when students are interested in writing in a specific genre, we immerse them in that genre. By studying the genre through many varied examples, students learn what other writers did to craft a particular piece. If we are teaching how to write poetry, we read poetry—lots of poetry. We read about the poets themselves and search for clues and writing tips. If we are teaching students to write a biography, we read biographies. And if we are teaching how to write an editorial, we read editorials. Again, we learn to write from other writers—if we listen carefully.

Literary Nonfiction

A genre that students enjoy reading and writing is literary nonfiction. It makes a great genre study. A picture book format presents lots of information in an engaging way. Although many of the books are difficult for the students to read independently, it is amazing how much they learn and how motivated they are to read them. These books are often good choices to use for reluctant readers and writers. We use them to encourage writers to write books that are fun to read and teach the reader something. Some examples are:

- *The Barn Owls*—Tony Johnston
- *The Birth of a Whale*—John Archambault
- *Crab Moon*—Ruth Horowitz
- *Fireboat*—Maira Kalman
- *Hello Ocean*—Pam Muñoz Ryan

- *Little Panda*—Joanne Ryder
- *Little Walrus Warning*—Carol Young
- *Mountain Dance*—Thomas Locker
- *One Tiny Turtle*—Nicola Davies
- *Out of the Ocean*—Debra Frasier

A genre study requires a guided inquiry approach, as we discussed earlier in the book. For example, when we try to improve report writing, we take the time to examine some nonfiction books together. Using the inquiry model, we see if students notice common text features and structures. They talk about why they think the writer chose to present information in a particular format. They consider if the genre matches the purpose of the writing. With guidance, students notice some common text features—the use of photographs, picture captions, table of contents, index, glossary, boldfaced words, charts, tables, headings, subheadings, and so on. They notice how the language and writing style differ from fiction. But we take our writers beyond just noticing. They consider the deliberate decisions the writer made as he crafted his work. They ask, and answer, "Why did the author do that?"

Our students ask questions of the text and of the author. The "right" answer is not what we're after. As our writers delve deeper into the genre, they show us what they can take away from this study and what they might apply to their own report writing. Their knowledge of genres and their use of mentor authors provide them the help they need to create their own product.

Genre Writing and State-mandated Writing Tests

It is important that you decide at your building or district level what writing genres to teach at each grade level. This is becoming more and more important as students prepare for state writing tests where we know that knowledge of certain genres will be expected of them. Most state-mandated writing tests take the form of narrative or expository writing. We believe that students will be successful on state writing tests if they are provided with:

- quality writing instruction
- regular opportunities to write
- choice of a variety of topics
- awareness of audience
- knowledge of writing genre
- awareness of how the purpose for writing influences the genre and form
- awareness of test format and procedures (for example, how to write a prompt)

Sample Genre Mini-lesson

Writing a Memoir

The purpose of this lesson is to show students how to write a memoir so they are not merely telling personal events but capturing a memory, sharing feelings related to it, and reflecting on it. The lesson that Barbara is leading here with a group of third graders takes place in the context of the inquiry unit "How do authors write well-crafted memoirs?"

BARBARA: *We've been exploring some books together the past week and talking about what they have in common. Let's take a look at them again. (She displays* Thunder Cake, When I Was Young in the Mountains, Fireflies!, The Relatives Came, Tar Beach, My Rotten Redheaded Older Brother, *and* Owl Moon.)

S: I liked *Fireflies!* because it reminded me of catching them last summer.

T: *I think we all like catching fireflies. But the author didn't just tell you about catching them. She helped you feel the excitement of catching them with friends. And she also let you feel how the boy felt as he later saw the fireflies dying in the jar and decided to let them free. What else did you notice about these books?*

S: Some of them seem to happen over just a day or a few hours—like *Thunder Cake.* It was just one storm. Oh, and where it happens—the setting—it seems obvious.

T: *That did seem like a short period of time with Patricia's grandmother helping her to get through a scary thunderstorm. The author also let you know how Trisha felt about storms. And I'm glad you noticed the setting of the stories. The setting is pretty important in visualizing a story.*

S: I think the author was writing about herself. That it probably really happened to her.

T: *I bet it did too. That's usually what we see in memoirs. These are experiences the writers had. What else do you notice about these books?*

S: In *The Relatives Came* it seemed like the time in the story was for weeks. But it was still a special time with relatives. I really like the pictures too.

T: *You're right. It did seem like it lasted over some weeks in the summer while they were waiting for the grape harvest.*

S: I like *Owl Moon* because it was just a time at night with a father, but I can't figure it out if it was it a boy or girl.

T: *What do you think . . .? Does it matter?*

S: Probably not, but I think it's a girl because it's written by Jane Yolen, and this could be something she did with her dad.

T: *That's good thinking. It seems like quite a few of these books are about special times with family members, and they seem to focus on just one special time or moment. These books are examples of memoirs. A memoir captures a time from our lives that is truly memorable, and it shares the feelings that go along with it. Listen again, a memoir captures time from our lives that is truly memorable, and it shares the feelings that go along with it.*

As you've been talking I've been writing down a few things on the chart that I'm hearing you say about memoirs. Let's take a look. We can always add to it.

Today I'm going to show you how you can capture a special moment so that you can write about it well. I like to use authors to help me with my writing, and I often use Patricia Polacco and Cynthia Rylant to help me. But this time I'm going to borrow what Jane Yolen did with her book Owl Moon. *I like the idea of her writing about a special night with Dad so I think I'll try that.*

Owl Moon *reminded me of a time that I went fishing with my dad. Really it was only one morning during a whole week of camping with my family. So instead of writing about the entire week of camping and all the stuff we did as a family all week long, I'm just going to write about that morning fishing with Dad.*

> ### What We Are Noticing About Memoirs
>
> - Author probably had the experience
> - You seem aware of the period of time
> - The setting seems obvious
> - You really remember it
> - It includes feelings

S: Why was it so special? It's just fishing.

T: *Because my sister and brother didn't go. I got up early one morning and noticed my dad was getting some fishing gear together. I asked him if he was going fishing all by himself, and that's when he asked if I'd like to join him. I thought it would be pretty neat. My mom and sister and brother weren't up yet so I thought I would go fishing just with my dad.*

S: Did you go out in a boat or just fish from a dock?

T: *In a boat. It was just a little row boat, but I remember how quiet and peaceful it was on the lake. I think I need to include that detail in my memoir. I want my readers to feel this same quiet. In* Owl Moon, *we were able to feel how quiet it was out there.*

(Barbara continues to talk with the class about the fishing experience to help the students relive it with her. Talking through a story before trying to write it can create great images and help rekindle memories. Talking is a powerful pre-writing tool that cannot be ignored.)

I want you to think about writing a memoir about a real special time. Think of some moment that you can capture in your head—where you can see it and remember it—and in your heart—where you can feel it.

S: Can I write about when my dad took me to his job for the day?

T: *Was that a real special time you can write about?*

S: I got to sit in his swivel chair and put my feet up on his desk.

T: *Wow! I can picture you doing that. That could be a great memoir. Slow down and tell many details and really try to help your reader feel the way you did that day.*

S: I want to write about when my dog had puppies.

T: *I bet that was really special. You probably have a lot of details you can include. Don't forget to tell us how many there were and what they looked like. Let's hear one more idea.*

S: I think I want to write about being a flower girl at my aunt's wedding. I felt like a bride walking down the aisle.

T: *You're already giving me a picture in my head. You can really include your feelings in your memoir and also some good description. As you begin to write, think about the things we've noticed in the other memoir books.*

It sounds like we're ready to get started. For those of you who are ready to start writing a memoir but are having a little trouble coming up with an idea, I want you to stay right here with me so I can give you a little extra help. The rest of you are ready to write.

Our work with the memoir genre would certainly not end here. This lesson will be followed with other mini-lessons about memoir writing. We'll look at more examples, see what else there is to discover and see how the student memoirs measure up. As the students draft their own memoirs, we'll conduct mini-lessons such as . . .

- "It made me feel happy" is not really evoking a feeling in the reader
- Writing interesting beginnings and endings
- Reading student drafts together and helping each other along
- Reading more examples and non-examples of the genre
- Ways to help your audience visualize
- Ways to help your audience empathize

Once again, it is this attention to depth, not "coverage" of the genre that makes a difference to our student writers.

Suggested Literature for Memoir Writing

- *All the Places to Love*—Patricia MacLachlan
- *The Baby Sister*—Tomie dePaola
- *Bigmama's*—Donald Crews
- *Birthday Presents*—Cynthia Rylant
- *A Chair for My Mother*—Vera B. Williams
- *David Goes to School*—David Shannon
- *Fireflies!*—Julie Brinckloe
- *Fishing in the Air*—Sharon Creech
- *Grandfather's Journey*—Allen Say
- *How My Parents Learned to Eat*—Ina R. Friedman
- *Just Us Women*—Jeannette Caines
- *Letting Swift River Go*—Jane Yolen
- *The Memory String*—Eve Bunting
- *Momma, Where Are You From?*—Marie Bradby
- *My Father's Hands*—Joanne Ryder
- *My Great Aunt Arizona*—Gail Houston
- *My Rotten Redheaded Older Brother*—Patricia Polacco
- *Owl Moon*—Jane Yolen
- *The Quilt Story*—Tomie dePaola
- *The Relatives Came*—Cynthia Rylant
- *Shortcut*—Donald Crews
- *Something to Remember Me By*—Susan V. Bosak
- *Storm in the Night*—Mary Stolz
- *Tar Beach*—Faith Ringgold
- *Tell Me a Story, Mama*—Angela Johnson
- *Thunder Cake*—Patricia Polacco
- *The Trip Back Home*—Janet S. Wong
- *When I Was Five*—Arthur Howard
- *When I Was Young in the Mountains*—Cynthia Rylant
- *Wilfrid Gordon MacDonald Partridge*—Mem Fox

Topics for Mini-lessons for Genre Writing

- Writing in the _____ genre

- Characteristics of the _____ genre

- Text structures in fiction

- Text structure in nonfiction

- Text features in fiction

- Text features in nonfiction

- Elements of literature

- Elements of poetry

- Role of illustrations, pictures, photographs

- Putting the illustrations and text together

- Including dialogue in your writing

- How to write using comparison and contrast

- Biographies vs. autobiographies

- Writing an autobiography

- Importance of details

- Researching for nonfiction writing

- Up-to-date information in nonfiction writing

- Making sure your facts are accurate

- Organizing and planning your writing

- Consider your audience

- Having a clear purpose for writing

- Note-taking

- Finding up-to-date and accurate information

- How to include new and unusual information

- Making your planning match your purpose and genre

- Sharing a new genre-writing attempt

- How reading assists our writing

- Including problems, events, and solutions in narrative writing

- How mentor authors can help us in a different genre

- Sequencing ideas and events

- Adding headings and subheadings to a report

- Choosing the best lead

- Choosing the best ending

- Descriptive writing

- Letting one's voice come through in writing

- How to write:

    Table of Contents
    Index
    Glossary

CHAPTER 10

Assessment Within the Writing Workshop

 THOUGHTFUL ASSESSMENT OF STUDENT WRITING LEADS TO IMPROVED WRITING. Assessment occurs while students are in the very act of writing and takes into account the entire writing process. In our Writing Workshops, we go far beyond assessing the final product. We view assessment as a powerful tool to help us grow as writers. Our most effective assessments are built on the students' trust in us. The trust has developed since the beginning of the year and extends over to other students. The writers know that if they take risks, they will get the support they need from this writing community.

During Writing Workshop, we are constantly on the lookout for students needing individual help. We meet individually with students in conferences, observe students conferring with one another, and listen carefully as writing is shared in the large group. We are constantly evaluating student work and determining their needs to make instructional decisions.

Opportunities for Observation and Assessment

Teachers often want to know how they can assess the overall work students do in Writing Workshop. Take a look at the following opportunities that are available to assess students in the various components of Writing Workshop.

Mini-lesson

- Student involvement and participation
- Responding to questioning or asking questions
- Demonstrating understanding of concepts
- Engagement in discussion

Independent Writing/Conferring

- Choice of topics for writing
- Number of pieces written
- Independent writing behaviors—time on task, engagement
- Involvement and level of discussion in conferences—with teacher and/or 'peers'

Sharing

- Confidence
- Willingness to share
- Oral language skills
- Listening skills
- Engagement in discussion
- Level of questions and responses

These opportunities address overall writing behaviors and experiences, not the final written product. We believe it's important to consider the students' behaviors in the workshop in addition to their actual writing. The following are ways we can fairly assess students in the workshop.

Anecdotal Records

While working with students one on one in a writing conference, we take anecdotal records on what we are addressing in the conference. Since each student is probably at a different point in the writing process, we want to be sure our records are clear and reflective of each student. We make sure to date our records so that we know how often we meet and what progress is made between conferences. Our notes are also specific about the focus of the conference. We shouldn't be covering the same skill every time we meet with a child. It's also a good idea to leave the student with a record of what was covered. A form in the student's writing folder that records conferences can take care of this. You can simply write what you taught that day and what you believe the child can be held accountable for in future writing. It can be as simple as "put page numbers on my writing" or a more challenging skill of "when using dialogue, begin a new paragraph for each speaker."

A form like the one below can be used by the student to keep track of what he specifically learned. We like the idea of including the title of the writing because it's a reminder of the piece he was working on at the time of the conference. It is also a helpful resource in the future if he needs to return to it for a reminder of what was done on a particular piece.

My Lessons From Conferences		
Date	**Title of Writing**	**What I Can Now Do in My Writing**
11/14	My Baby Brother	write a dedication page
11/23	Poisonous Snakes	write picture captions
11/29	Poisonous Snakes	use commas in a series
12/7	Camping	include dialogue

▲ *An easy form to hold students accountable for what they learn about writing*

Observation Checklists

Checklists can provide a quick and easy way to assess writing behaviors. We can easily individualize them so that they have all the attributes we are evaluating. For example, if we are assessing student behaviors during independent writing time, then we include on the checklist what we feel is important. See the following checklist.

Independent Writing Time

Student Name	On-task behavior; Engaged in personal writing	Appropriate behavior and discussion with teacher in conference	Assists others when appropriate	Portfolio is complete	Appropriate interaction with peers in conferences	Evidence of variety of topics and/or genre	Evidence of application of instruction

▲ *A checklist to keep track of writing behaviors*

Rubrics

Rubrics provide us with a way to assess key elements using specific performance criteria. It is an excellent form of assessment for writing because it allows us the opportunity to determine the standards by which we are to judge writing behaviors and performance. When we share these standards with our students (and their parents), they know the expectations.

Rubrics can be used to provide direction for the writing so that the writer knows the expectations for the task. In this way, the student has a guide for what is expected for a specific genre. Rubrics can also be evaluative in nature. The writer is given specific criteria that explain how the writing will be graded or scored. Rubrics can be as formal or informal, and as general or specific as you want them.

Rubrics are extremely adaptable. Some are developed at the state level for state writing tests, some within a school district so there is uniformity from school to school, and some at the school or classroom level. Within the classroom, teachers often involve students in the creation of rubrics. Students have a vested interest in the evaluation when they help create the assessment tool.

With that said, we need to keep the use of rubrics in check. Not every piece of writing has to be evaluated using a rubric. In fact, not every piece of writing should be evaluated. If our students are writing as much as we expect, then there is no way to assess every piece of writing. Also, it is unfair to expect students to always be at their best. But we do need to look at their portfolios and judge the growth and progress they have made over the year.

We have included two different kinds of rubrics. The first rubric enables us to assess our students' overall participation in Writing Workshop. By looking at each component of the Workshop, we determine each student's level of performance. This assessment is usually done twice a marking period.

This next rubric assesses a written product. In order to create these rubrics, first the indicators were determined—composing, craft, and conventions. Then the expectations for each indicator were established. Two variations of the rubric are included: one for primary and one for intermediate.

Total Score _____

Assessment Rubric for Writing Workshop

Writing Workshop Component	Student Behaviors	4 Clearly evident	3 Mostly evident	2 Some evidence	1 Little evidence
Mini-lesson	Actively engaged and participates in the lesson. Asks questions and responds to others. Demonstrates an understanding of the lesson.				
Independent Writing	Views self as a writer. Uses the writing process and takes times to plan and develop the writing. Works independently and remains on task. Writes on a variety of topics.				
Conferring With Teacher	Involved in conference discussion. Able to articulate and use language appropriate to writing. Aware of where he/she is in the writing process. Accepts constructive criticism. Able to set goals for self.				
Conferring With Peers	Involved in appropriate conversations with peer(s). Able to be constructive and assist others while also being able to accept help when needed. Remains on task working with others.				
Project Completion	Student completes written projects. Able to find topics to write about. Tries a variety of genres.				
Share Time	Demonstrates confidence and willingness to share writing. Shows good oral language and listening skills. Engaged in conversation on writing. Asks appropriate questions and responds to others.				

Assessment Rubric for Writing • Primary

	4	3	2	1
Composing	▪ Writing is well-organized with a beginning, middle, ending ▪ Stays on topic throughout the paper ▪ Elaboration contains interesting word choices for specific examples and descriptions	▪ Writing shows some organization with a beginning, middle, ending ▪ Mostly stays on topic ▪ Some elaboration, although word choices are not specific	▪ Writing is not well organized and is missing a beginning or ending ▪ Tends to digress and write off topic ▪ Little attempt at elaboration	▪ No evidence of organization ▪ Does not stay on topic ▪ Does not elaborate
Craft	▪ Words have been carefully chosen and specific ▪ Sentences show variety and fluency ▪ Writing shows an obvious structure	▪ Words were chosen for the topic ▪ Some evidence of sentence variety ▪ Some attempt at structuring the writing	▪ Words are general and not well thought out ▪ Little evidence of sentence variety ▪ Little attempt to structure writing	▪ Words are not specific ▪ No variety of sentences. ▪ Some are vague or awkward. ▪ No structure to writing
Conventions	▪ All sentences are complete ▪ Correct use of capitalization ▪ Uses proper punctuation ▪ All "core" words are spelled correctly	▪ Most sentences are complete ▪ Most words capitalized correctly, but some capitals are found in the middle of words (doG, rEd) ▪ Most of the time uses correct punctuation ▪ Most "core" words are spelled correctly	▪ Some sentences are complete ▪ Inconsistent use of capitalization ▪ Sometimes uses punctuation ▪ Some "core" words are spelled correctly	▪ Sentences are incomplete ▪ No attempt at capitalization ▪ No attempt at punctuation ▪ Numerous spelling errors including those that are "core" words

Assessment Rubric for Writing • Intermediate

	4	3	2	1
Composing	▪ Writing is well-organized with a clear beginning, middle, ending ▪ Stays on topic throughout the paper ▪ Elaboration contains specific examples and descriptions ▪ Point of view is consistent	▪ Writing shows some organization with a beginning, middle, ending ▪ Mostly stays on topic ▪ Some elaboration although words are not specific ▪ Point of view is usually consistent	▪ Writing is not well organized and is missing a beginning or ending ▪ Tends to digress and write off topic ▪ Little attempt at elaboration ▪ Point of view changes	▪ No evidence of organization ▪ Does not stay on topic ▪ Does not elaborate ▪ Point of view is not clear
Craft	▪ Words have been carefully chosen and specific ▪ Sentences show variety and fluency ▪ Writing shows an obvious structure ▪ Writer's voice is clearly evident ▪ Tone of the writing is clearly evident	▪ Words were chosen for the topic ▪ Some evidence of sentence variety ▪ Some attempt at structuring the writing ▪ Writer's voice is mostly evident ▪ Tone of the writing is mostly evident	▪ Words are general and not well thought out ▪ Little evidence of sentence variety ▪ Little attempt to structure writing ▪ Writer's voice is somewhat evident ▪ Tone of the writing is somewhat evident	▪ Words are not specific ▪ No variety of sentences. Some are vague or awkward. ▪ No structure to writing ▪ Writer's voice is not evident ▪ Tone of the writing is not evident
Conventions	▪ All sentences are complete ▪ Always uses proper grammar ▪ Correct use of capitalization ▪ Uses proper punctuation ▪ All words are spelled correctly ▪ Paper is clearly legible for the reader	▪ Most sentences are complete ▪ Mostly uses proper grammar ▪ Most words capitalized correctly ▪ Most of the time uses correct punctuation ▪ Most words are spelled correctly ▪ Paper is mostly legible for the reader	▪ Some sentences are complete ▪ Sometimes uses proper grammar ▪ Inconsistent use of capitalization ▪ Sometimes uses punctuation ▪ Many misspelled words ▪ Paper is somewhat legible for the reader	▪ Sentences are incomplete ▪ Does not use proper grammar ▪ No attempt at capitalization ▪ No attempt at punctuation ▪ Numerous spelling errors including "core" words ▪ Paper is not legible

Student Self-assessments

Rubrics and checklists are valuable tools we use to assess student writing. But we must also consider what the students can do themselves to evaluate their own writing. We allow time for students to look at their overall body of work, to reflect, and to set goals. There are times when we must step back and have the writers reflect and self-evaluate. They can look over their portfolios and determine what merits our time and energy to evaluate. Take a look at the following student's self-evaluation form for intermediate-level students.

Self-Evaluation of Student Selected Writing

Name:

Date:

Title:

Genre:

- What is your purpose/goal/audience for this writing?
- What are the strengths in this piece of writing?
- What mentor author(s) did you use?
- What craft did you try in this writing?
- New goal for future writing:

The following self-evaluation form can be used for primary students—whether they respond in writing or verbally within the context of an assessment conference.

Self-Evaluation of Student Selected Writing

Name:

Date:

Title:

- What do you think makes this a good piece of writing?
- What did you do that you really like in your writing?
- Did a mentor author help you craft your writing?
- What is your goal for your next piece of writing?

At least once (but preferably twice) a marking period, we meet our students in individual "rubric conferences." We make the rubric for Writing Workshop available to students prior to these conferences. For about a week (so we can get to everyone), instead of our typical conferences, we meet with students to complete a rubric together. We talk about overall progress and what the student is doing to meet his goals. Often, we use this time to set new goals. After this conference, students have a clear picture of what they are doing well and what they need to be working on.

Personal Writing Goals

By following student work in conferences and share time, teachers are able to pinpoint a few ways the writing can be improved. We create small, reasonable goals that students can remember and articulate. These goals are posted in student folders and sent home to parents at report card time. We expect all students to actively work toward meeting their goals and receiving new goals at the end of each marking period. Goals can be as simple as, "I can remember to add details to my pictures." Or, as intricate as, "I can remember to check for and revise my run-on sentences." Goals might be as global as, "I can reread my work before I start each day." Or, a goal might be as specific as, "I can remember to use I in compound subjects." Goals are always stated using the "I can" phrase. They do not mean "maybe you should try," but that you will follow through. Typically goals are first created after the first few weeks of Writing Workshop. Students usually have two or three goals. We type them out and print them on labels, three copies of each. One label is affixed to an explanatory parent letter, one label goes in teacher notes, and one label goes right in the student's writing folder. With luck, each student receives a new set of goals at the end of the quarter. If a goal is not met, we keep it where it is.

The following are examples of goals for students. They are, for the most part, listed in increasing writing ability. Some goals are appropriate for all levels.

- I can work more slowly on my illustrations.
- I can remember to put my name on all my writing.
- I can add labels to my pictures.
- I can say words slowly and write all the sounds I hear.
- I can remember spaces between my words.
- I can check for correct capitals.
- I can check for correct punctuation.
- I can use the word wall to check my sight words.
- I can remember to include a clear beginning, middle, and end.
- I can try to have a plan in my head for a story before writing.

- I can think about our mentor authors and try to craft my work.
- I can use an interesting story structure for my stories.
- I can use all of my writing time wisely.
- I can reread to be sure my story is about only one thing.
- I can try to think of more to say about the topic.
- I can remember that my audience needs me to be interesting.
- I can make sure I am using *a* and *an* correctly.
- I can include dialogue.
- I can vary sentence structure in my writing.

This list is by no means exhaustive. Each student may require different goals, or you may have many students who need to work on the same goals. To be most effective, goals must be personal, represent small steps in writing growth, and be fully understood by the student.

State-mandated Writing Assessments

Our fifth graders know the importance of the spring state writing tests. All that they have learned comes together for this one-day test when they are asked to write to a given prompt. They are prepared and know they are to consider the purpose of the task and the audience. While they have been exposed to the craft of good writers, they also know there are some things they should and should not include in such a writing test. For example, they may love the way Cynthia Rylant uses fragments or Libba Moore Gray creates her own words. But they would rightfully hesitate to use these techniques when asked to write in a more formal manner on a state test. They know that, in this case, their audience is not as interested in risk-taking or creative ways with words. Their audience wants to know what the writer knows about complete thoughts, main ideas and supportive details, and other grammatical skills.

We believe in teaching students to write well, in exposing them to the good writing of others, and in giving them multiple opportunities to write. We know that the best readers read, and the best writers write. They learn to write well because they have numerous opportunities to write—and the guidance to write well.

Just as we prepare our students for the state reading tests by building their reading stamina, we do the same for writing. Students should be able to write fluently. In most cases, the writing should come easily for them. They may not like the prompt given to them, but they know how to deal with it.

Writing to Prompts

While Writing Workshop usually affords students opportunities to write on topics of their choice, there are times when we expect them to write on a given topic—typically what is expected of them on state tests. These on-demand topics show up in other testing situations, e.g., college-entrance or job applications. So although it may not represent all that we value in writing, writing to a prompt has its place in the real world. We would do our students an injustice if we did not prepare them for it. We introduce this type of writing as just another genre—the testing genre.

In order for students to do their best on this type of writing, we must fully prepare them. Just as we demonstrate writing behaviors for other genres, we model writing to a prompt. We show the decisions we make as we decide the form our writing will take. When thinking aloud, we're sure to show students how we are constantly asking ourselves the following questions:

Our school has designated school-wide writing days when all the students are asked to write on a given topic; e.g., "My favorite animal is . . . " After this writing task, the teachers meet in grade-level teams. Using rubrics adapted from those developed at the state level, the teachers score the papers together and decide what constitutes average, above average, and below average writing. With teachers evaluating each other students' writings, they share in decisions to improve classroom writing instruction.

■ What am I being asked to write about?

■ What form should this take?

■ Who will be reading this?

■ How should I plan my writing?

■ Is there anything in particular I have to include in my writing?

■ How much time should I spend on planning?

■ Am I ready to write my draft?

■ Do I think I've written enough?

■ Have I addressed the prompt?

■ Can I improve some of my word choices?

■ Is there variety in my sentences and paragraphs?

■ Have I checked my work?

In addition, we also model how to do all of this in one sitting—just the way they'll be expected to complete the assignment. After we have written our essay, we take the time to score it with our students using the state rubric. This reflection time helps them see how the writing matches up with the scoring criteria.

Again, a caution. Writing instruction whose sole aim is writing assessment denies our students powerful opportunities to grow as writers. Since we receive limited feedback from the state writing test and because it comes at the end of the year, the tests do little to help improve student writing in the year they are given. Thus, it is necessary to rely on the students' ongoing writing to help them improve as writers.

Determining Grades

Grading writing is not like grading a math assignment or a science test. Although we may hesitate to put a grade on a piece of writing, it is inevitable that we must. In order to do so, we need to know our expectations, we need to set the criteria for determining a grade, and we need to communicate them to our students and parents. We must also keep in mind the effort, progress, and the overall body of work, not just a final product. If we can balance our criteria for determining grades with the students' self-assessments, we will indeed create better, more reflective writers.

Assessment of student writing provides us with the information we need to make the best instructional decisions. Through this assessment, the decisions we make help move our students forward. With our evaluation and their self-reflection, they grow as writers and continue to show us all they can do.

CHAPTER 11

Writing Throughout the Day
and Throughout the Year

 S WE WERE REVISING AND ENHANCING OUR WRITING INSTRUCTION, WE MET WITH A COUPLE OF SETBACKS AND FRUSTRATIONS. Mostly though, we saw true progress. Students wrote with more feeling. They cared more about their work. There was evidence through their own writing and through testing that our young writers understood the craft of writing. Parents and administrators were amazed by what the kids were able to accomplish. But what really "wowed" us was the students' behavior outside of the Writing Workshop. Students, of their own accord, were writing at home and bringing their work in to share with the class. Many groups would take paper and clipboards out to recess because they wanted to keep writing. And some others, after witnessing an unusual event, would comment, "That would make a great story!" We knew we were on our way to accomplishing what we set out to do—go beyond having students write and nurture them to *be* writers.

In the beginning, we kept coming back to the notion of real readers and real writers. Reading and writing are necessary in our lives and in our world. We wanted to lift reading and writing out of just classrooms. We wanted our students to see them as invaluable communication tools. One of the best ways to show our students that writing is not just a school subject is to help them see how writing extends beyond the confines of the actual Writing Workshop. Our Workshop, then, is not a stand-alone entity. It is but a part, albeit a large part, of a structure that supports and nurtures these writers.

There are many ways to support our budding authors outside of the Writing Workshop. We must teach writing throughout the day, in all subjects. We must celebrate success, in big ways and in small ways. We need to work hard to sustain momentum and enthusiasm throughout the entire year. We must consistently raise expectations. And throughout all of this, whenever possible, we must invite parents into this process. They are often our students' best cheerleaders.

Writing Instruction Outside of the Workshop

Many teachers see the need and the value of writing in the content areas. What we often do not see though is the clear connection we must make between writing in social studies and the writing done during Writing Workshop. We need to be sure we present information in similar ways, using similar terms. The writing assignment should be open-ended enough so that it could be completed during the Writing Workshop. Making distinctions between writing for science and writing during writing times only muddies the water for our writers. Good writing and good writing instruction are appropriate throughout the entire school day. Students should always be held to the same standards, regardless of whether the topic is assigned or self-selected. Writing is writing is writing. And, good writing is always good writing.

It's important to remember these opportunities for more writing instruction and practice during the day:

- **Morning Message**—Usually seen in primary classrooms, this is a time for both modeling and guided practice. Each day students can practice using the entire writing process, from choosing a topic to drafting with sound spelling and use of the word wall, to revising and editing.

- **Daily Edit**—This often takes the place of the morning message in intermediate classrooms. This exercise gives students a chance to practice analyzing someone else's writing and making appropriate corrections. If done independently it should be checked together fairly soon after completion. Students should never be required to copy a sentence that contains errors. It's much more appropriate for the sentence to be typed out on individual copies.

❋ **Reading Journals or Responses**—Many students are asked to do some writing in conjunction with their daily reading. Students should be encouraged to always apply what they are learning during Writing Workshop to their reading responses. If you expect something in their written stories, you should definitely expect it in their journals.

❋ **Learning Logs**—These are used by all grade levels so that students can record their synthesis of a certain topic. By helping students become familiar with such a format, we help them to see how writing new information down helps us remember and organize our thoughts. This powerful tool helps students begin to think about note-taking and summarizing.

❋ **Read-Alouds**—Students are read to many times outside of Writing Workshop. Once writers start to understand what it means to think about how a book is crafted, they'll want to talk about all books that way. To a certain extent, we need to let them, until you find they are talking more about how the book was written than what the book was about. In a social studies read-aloud, this is not helpful. We'll remind our students that the main reason we're looking at this particular story is to learn something about the social studies topic. And, we'll offer to bring the same book out during a writing time in order to discuss its craft in further detail.

Sustaining Momentum Throughout the Year

When we talk with teachers about the importance of keeping the Workshop time predictable, we're often met with some resistance. "I can't do anything the same all year long." "I just know my students will lose interest." While there's always a risk of students and teachers getting bored, we find that the growing repertoire of writing craft and ideas seems to keep classes moving until the last days of school. However, we do have to be mindful of this risk and actively pursue student engagement.

When we reflect on what it is that actually keeps us moving throughout the year, it's hard to pinpoint one or two things that we, as teachers, are doing. The energy to push forward, clearly, comes from our writers and their accomplishments. We follow their lead. We see their writing grow stronger and stronger and we feel the need to keep pushing. We look at a student's work in November, marvel at what he's accomplished, and imagine how fabulous his work will be in May. We do not accept that some students just "plateau." There is always a way to improve.

We recommend a few ways that can help sustain momentum throughout the year:

❋ Remember how important time for sharing actually is. We tell our students over and over again to think about audience. We cannot, therefore, take that audience away. Most students love to share, and they enjoy learning from their peers. Students learn who is good at what, and they start to look forward to the next piece written by their friends. We must remember to honor this need for the company of our friends by allowing time for learning from and helping out others.

❋ Follow through with goal-setting. We've mentioned how helpful it is to set both small, daily goals and larger, quarterly goals for the students. Setting the goals, however, is really only just the beginning. Unless all students are actively striving to meet these goals, it doesn't really matter whether the goals exist or not. Students should be able to articulate their goals at any time. They should know what they need to do to meet the goal. Most importantly, we need to be there to applaud when the goal is met. In this way, we set up a structure that is always moving forward. When students know that they are working toward something, they strive to get there. Without the experience of consistently getting better by meeting their goals, students can get stuck and just spin their wheels during writing time. We've had success with a simple bulletin board in the hallway that acknowledges all this forward movement. The bulletin board was titled, "Look at who's shooting for the stars." We ran off a bunch of stars on yellow paper, labeled "Now I can . . ." We met with students in conferences and when it was clear a goal was met, we handed the student a star. He or she filled it out, and we hung it up together. It was very little effort on our part, but it was a good way to recognize the huge amount of effort on their part.

❋ Even with all the strong teaching within our Workshops, we know that we will never help bring about substantive change within one of our students unless we make the curriculum personal. For this reason, we advocate a great deal of self-reflection time within the Writing Workshop. Students need time to look

A public celebration of goals met

through their work and form opinions. They need time to see what they did well and what they should have done differently. Of course, we show our students how to do this. We help them to begin looking at their own work more critically. We model self-talk that inspires growth. At least once a quarter, students must sit down and review their portfolios. This process enables them to actually see their own growth, or in some cases, lack of growth. Even though they hear us say all the time that they are getting better and better, what really keeps the momentum going is when each student sees it for herself.

* Students must know that we have ever-climbing expectations for each of them. We'd be remiss if we didn't acknowledge that for all our talk of "just see what happens, follow their lead, and honor all attempts," we still hold high expectations for all of our writers. We still feel the push of benchmark assessments and objectives. We are utterly realistic about what it is each child must leave us with each year. And so, relentlessly, we push a little each day. We listen and watch carefully. We know who needs extra assistance and with what, and we know to plan accordingly. The trick is to make sure that the students see themselves as writers. We're clear in our expectations—"This is what's required of all good writers, and you are all good writers." As their teachers, we strive each day to prove this to them. "You are good writers, and together we'll work so that you become even better writers. You can, you will, I expect it." We do believe that without this relentless push toward higher expectations we'd all become bored, and our Writing Workshop would devolve into just another writing class.

* And of course, we're realistic in the fact that we know we play an important role in the atmosphere of the room. Their writing development is important to us. In many ways, we are quite passionate about it. We know that our enthusiasm is contagious, and we play to that advantage. Presentation is everything, and we're certain to try to make every aspect of the writing process as enticing as we can. Even when it comes to lessons on apostrophes or dictionary skills, it's all in how you spin it!

Celebrating Writing Accomplishments

One of the reasons our Writing Workshops are so successful is that they become so personal to the students. You can't really study for a writing test the way you would a math or science test. Writing is about putting yourself out there and giving others a glimpse into who you are. It entails risk-taking and confidence. Because we are asking so much of our writers each and every day, we go out of our way to celebrate their hard work and dedication.

We celebrate in small ways each time we announce in the middle of independent writing time, "Writers, hold everything for a second, you have got to hear what Dashaun has done with his story . . ." We celebrate in predictable ways each day at share time when we elevate writers to the status of teacher when we say to the class, "What can you learn about good writing from what Alex has just shared with you?" And, we celebrate in big ways when we take the time to plan a big occasion solely for the purpose of showcasing and honoring the work of our writers. Take a look at some of the ways we can celebrate with a bang.

- Host an informal writers' meeting—Invite another class into your room and invite students to find a buddy who will share their writing.

- Have students polish one piece of writing to be given as a gift.

- Host an authors' tea—Invite parents to an afternoon of tea, lemonade, and cookies. Students can read a favorite piece aloud.

- Open a writers' museum—writers can prepare an exhibit by selecting their favorites for display. Authors are available during browsing time for questions and book signing.

- Host a coffeehouse poetry day—Transform your room into a neighborhood coffee house, complete with "open mic" opportunities, when students come up to the microphone to perform original poetry.

While we try to have one big event at least once during the year, it might make sense to end each inquiry unit or each marking period with a larger celebration. With any of the above ideas, be certain to include the students in the planning process. After all, it's their work on display.

Communicating With Parents

In the best possible world, the conversation about strong writing should continue outside of the school building. Although we know this won't always happen, we like to structure our communication with parents and families so that this conversation might be possible. You want parents to ask questions of their child, and to praise their child when he has met a goal, acknowledging all the effort it took to get there. And perhaps most importantly, you want parents to honor all the attempts the young writer is making. Most parents are not prepared to do this right away. They need our help and guidance in this area. There are several ways we try to keep our families in the loop. The idea is to help parents see what you are attempting to do in your writing classroom. Take a look at some possible ways of educating your parents.

- Have a brief introduction to Writing Workshop in your back-to-school letter.

- Together with other teachers, plan an evening workshop for parents where they can learn about the writing process, grade level expectations, and ways parents can help with writing at home.

- Make sure your rubrics are clearly worded so that when parents look at the writing, it is easy to tell what was done well and what needs to be worked on.

- Send notices to parents when students meet their goals. And inform parents when new goals are set. Emphasize the importance of using the same language and working toward the same goals both at home and at school.

- About every quarter or so, students usually need to clean out their portfolio. Send home some writing attached to a letter that explains what's been happening in the writing class and what sort of skills you've been working on.

- Update parents about Writing Workshop mini-lesson topics in your regular weekly or monthly newsletters.

Well informed parents can be great allies. It's always wonderful to hear a parent marvel about how, during bedtime story, their seven-year-old stopped and said, "Don't you just love the way the author crafted that!"

We love to use the book *ish* by Peter H. Reynolds when meeting with parents. Often parents need help honoring the developmental level of their writers. We use this story to begin our conversation about realistic expectations.

A Reflection . . .

As we look back on the journey we have taken with this book,
we hope you see the possibilities as you revisit your Writing Workshop.
Our students are capable of being great writers,
and it is up to us to lead them down that path.

In this age of state testing, it is too easy to get caught up
in teaching students just to write for the test.
But real writers don't write to tests.
Real writers know that writing spills over into all aspects of our days.
As teachers, we need to develop writers who have skills
that go beyond test taking and even beyond the confines
of the Writing Workshop.

Writing is a way of life, and through writing,
students can truly express who they are.
Start a new journey with your young writers
and see how far they can go.

Appendix

Anchor Texts

T IS IMPOSSIBLE TO LIST ALL OF THE WONDERFUL BOOKS THAT WE HAVE DISCOVERED AND USED OVER THE YEARS.

However, there are some books that are our anchor texts, those books that we consider our must-haves that we keep returning to over and over. There are also some authors who we seem to be drawn to frequently.

The following book lists are intended to get you started. You will notice they are predominantly picture books. We find picture books invaluable because they contain great writing and techniques that can easily be pointed out. You will soon find yourself noticing writer's craft and adding to your collection of must-haves.

Word Choice

We use the following titles because of the way they are written. They include beautiful language, interesting word choice, and/or unique sentence construction.

Baker, Alan—*Two Tiny Mice*

Bunting, Eve—*The Secret Place*

Burleigh, Robert—*Home Run*

Chall, Marsha Wilson—*Up North at the Cabin*

Curtis, Gavin—*The Bat Boy and His Violin*

Fraustino, Lisa Rose—*The Hickory Chair*

Gray, Libba Moore—*My Mama Had a Dancing Heart*

Hundal, Nancy—*Camping*

Johnston, Tony—*The Barn Owls*

Joose, Barbara—*I Love You the Purplest*

Locker, Thomas—*Mountain Dance*

London, Jonathan—*Puddles*

MacLachlan, Patricia—
    All the Places to Love
    Painting the Wind

Nicholls, Judith—*Billywise*

Paulsen, Gary—*Canoe Days*

Pearson, Susan—*Silver Morning*

Ryan, Pam Muñoz—*Hello Ocean*

Ryder, Joanne—*My Father's Hands*

Rylant, Cynthia—
    In November
    Night in the Country
    Scarecrow
    The Relatives Came
    Tulip Sees America
    The Whales
    When I Was Young in the Mountains

Stolz, Mary—*Storm in the Night*

Wood, Douglas—*A Quiet Place*

Yolen, Jane—
    Miz Berlin Walks
    Owl Moon
    Welcome to the Green House

Text Format and Structure

These books are included because their text format or structure makes them unique. When students read these books, they notice the different structure, how the text may be formatted, and even the use of punctuation.

Appelt, Kathi—*Bubba and Beau, Best Friends*

Bond, Rebecca—*This Place in the Snow*

Brown, Margaret Wise—*The Important Book*

Carlstrom, Nancy White—

    Goodbye Geese

    What Does the Sky Say?

    Where Does the Night Hide?

Crum, Shutta—*The Bravest of the Brave*

Fitch, Sheree—*No Two Snowflakes*

Frazee, Marla—*Roller Coaster*

Gray, Libba Moore—

    Dear Willie Rudd

    My Mama Had a Dancing Heart

Green, Donna—*My Little Artist*

Hopkinson, Deborah—*Fannie in the Kitchen*

Martin, Bill Jr.—*Knots on a Counting Rope*

Martin, Jacqueline Briggs—*On Sand Island*

Ryder, Joanne—*My Father's Hands*

Rylant, Cynthia—

    In November

    Long Night Moon

    Scarecrow

    Tulip Sees America

Sams, Carl—

    Lost in the Woods

    Stranger in the Woods

Stewart, Sarah—*The Gardener*

Stilton, Geronimo—Geronimo Stilton books

Stojic, Manya—*Rain*

Wiesmuller, Dieter—*In the Blink of an Eye*

Willems, Mo—*Knuffle Bunny*

Mood or Tone

The following books can be used when you are trying to show your students how writers create a mood or tone in their books. Sometimes they are light and humorous, while at other times they are much more serious and somber.

Bahr, Mary—*The Memory Box*

Base, Graeme—*The Water Hole*

Bradby, Marie—*More Than Anything Else*

Brinckloe, Julie—*Fireflies!*

Bunting, Eve—

    Fly Away Home

    Smoky Night

    Swan in Love

    Train to Somewhere

    The Wall

Cooper, Melrose—*Gettin' Through Thursday*

Fox, Mem—*Wilfrid Gordon MacDonald Partridge*

Frazee, Marla—*Roller Coaster*

Gray, Libba Moore—

    Dear Willie Rudd

    My Mama Had a Dancing Heart

Hesse, Karen—*Out of the Dust* (chapter book)

Johnston, Angela—*The Leaving Morning*

Laminack, Lester—*The Sunsets of Miss Olivia Wiggins*

Mathis, Sharon Bell—*Sidewalk Story* (chapter book)

MacLachlan, Patricia and Emily MacLachlan Charest—

    Once I Ate a Pie

Munsch, Robert—*Mmm, Cookies* (almost any Robert Munsch book)

Pilkey, Dav—*Dog Breath*

Rylant, Cynthia Rylant—

    The Great Gracie Chase

    The Relatives Came

Viorst, Judith—

    Alexander and the Terrible, Horrible, No Good, Very Bad Day

    Earrings!

Passage of Time

Writers use different techniques when they want to move a story through time—either through the use of illustrations or text. We have included the following selection because these books are helpful to those students whose stories go on and on and on. Even an easy-to-read book like *Henry and Mudge: The First Book* uses illustrations to show how Mudge grows up.

Bunting, Eve—*The Blue and the Gray*

Fraustino, Lisa Rowe—*The Hickory Chair*

Haseley, Dennis—*A Story for Bear*

Hest, Amy—*When Jessie Came Across the Sea*

Johnson, Paul Brett J. and Celeste Lewis—*Lost*

LaMarche, Jim—*The Raft*

Polacco, Patricia—

    My Rotten Redheaded Older Brother

    Thunder Cake

Rylant, Cynthia—*Henry and Mudge: The First Book*

Simont, Marc—*The Stray Dog*

Stevens, Janet—*My Big Dog*

Ward, Cindy—*Cookie's Week*

Professional Resources

Atwell, Nancie. *In the Middle*. Portsmouth, NH: Boynton/Cook-Heinemann, 1987.

Atwell, Nancie. *In the Middle* (2nd ed.). Portsmouth, NH: Heinemann, 1998.

Avery, Carol. *. . . And With a Light Touch*. Portsmouth, NH: Heinemann, 2002.

Calkins, Lucy McCormick. *The Art of Teaching Writing*. Portsmouth, NH: Heinemann, 1994.

Dorfman, Lynne R. & Cappelli, Rose. *Mentor Texts*. Portland, ME: Stenhouse, 2007

Fletcher, Ralph. *What a Writer Needs*. Portsmouth, NH: Heinemann, 1993.

Fountas, Irene C. & Pinnell, Gay Su. *Guiding Readers and Writers*. Portsmouth, NH: Heinemann, 2001.

Graves, Donald H. & Kittle, Penny. *Inside Writing: How to Teach the Details of Craft*. Portsmouth, NH: Heinemann, 2005.

Laminack, Lester L. & Wadsworth, Reba M. *Learning Under the Influence of Language and Literature*. Portsmouth, NH: Heinemann, 2006.

Lindfors, Judith Wells. *Children's Inquiry*. New York: Teachers College Press, 1999.

McCarthy, Tara. *Teaching Genre*. New York: Scholastic Inc., 1996.

Orehovec, Barbara & Alley, Marybeth. *Revisiting the Reading Workshop*. New York: Scholastic Inc., 2003.

Ray, Katie Wood. *About the Authors*. Portsmouth, NH: Heinemann, 2004.

Ray, Katie Wood. *What You Know by Heart*. Portsmouth, NH: Heinemann, 2002.

Ray, Katie Wood. *Wondrous Words*. Urbana, IL: National Council of Teachers of English, 1999.

Routman, Regie. *Writing Essentials*. Portsmouth, NH: Heinemann, 2005.

Recommended Children's Literature for Writing Workshop

Abercrombie, Barbara. *Charlie Anderson*. New York: Aladdin Paperbacks, 1990.

Ada, Alma Flor. *Dear Peter Rabbit*. New York: Aladdin Paperbacks, 1994.

Adler, David. *My Writing Day*. Katonah, NY: Richard C. Owens, 1999.

Appelt, Kathi. *Bubba and Beau, Best Friends*. San Diego: Harcourt, Inc., 2002.

Archambault, John. *The Birth of a Whale*. Parsippany, NJ: Silver Press, 1996.

Avi. *Poppy*. New York: Harper Trophy, 1995.

Bahr, Mary. *The Memory Box*. Morton Grove, IL: Albert Whitman & Company, 1992.

Baker, Alan. *Two Tiny Mice*. New York: Scholastic Inc., 1990.

Base, Graeme. *The Water Hole*. New York: Harry N. Abrams, Inc., Publishers, 2001.

Bloom, Suzanne. *A Splendid Friend, Indeed*. Honesdale, PA: Boyds Mill Press, 2005.

Bond, Rebecca. *This Place in the Snow*. New York: Dutton Children's Books, 2004.

Borden, Louise. A. *Lincoln and Me*. New York: Scholastic Inc., 1999.

Borden, Louise. *The Day Eddie Met the Author*. New York: Margaret K. McElderry Books, 2001.

Bosak, Susan V. *Something to Remember Me By*. New York: Scholastic Inc., 1999.

Boyd, Candy Dawson. *Circle of Gold*. New York: Scholastic Inc., 1984.

Bradby, Marie. *Momma, Where Are You From?* New York: Orchard Books, 2000.

Bradby, Marie. *More Than Anything Else*. New York: Orchard Books, 1995.

Brinckloe, Julie. *Fireflies!* New York: Macmillan, 1985.

Brown, Marc. *Arthur Writes a Story.* New York: Scholastic Inc., 1996.

Brown, Margaret Wise. *The Important Book.* New York: The Trumpet Club, 1949.

Bunting, Eve. *The Blue and the Gray.* New York: Scholastic Inc., 1996.

Bunting, Eve. *Fly Away Home.* New York: Clarion Books, 1991.

Bunting, Eve. *The Memory String.* New York: Clarion Books, 2000.

Bunting, Eve. *Once Upon a Time.* Katonah, NY: Richard C. Owens, 1995.

Bunting, Eve. *A Secret Place.* New York: Clarion Books, 1996.

Bunting, Eve. *Smoky Night.* San Diego: Harcourt Brace, 1995.

Bunting, Eve. *Swan in Love.* New York: Atheneum Books for Young Readers, 2000.

Bunting, Eve. *Train to Somewhere.* New York: Scholastic Inc., 1996.

Bunting, Eve. *The Wall.* New York: Clarion Books, 1990.

Bunting Eve. *The Wednesday Surprise.* New York: Clarion Books, 1989.

Burleigh, Robert. *Home Run.* San Diego: Harcourt Brace & Company, 1998.

Caines, Jeannette. *Just Us Women.* New York: Scholastic Inc., 1982.

Cannon, Janell. *Stellaluna.* San Diego: Harcourt Brace, 1993.

Carlstrom, Nancy White. *Good-bye Geese.* New York: Scholastic Inc., 1991.

Carlstrom, Nancy White. *What Does the Sky Say?* Grand Rapids, MI: Eerdmans Books for Young Readers, 2001.

Carlstrom, Nancy White. *Where Does the Night Hide?* New York: Macmillan, 1990.

Carrick, Carol. *Mothers Are Like That.* New York: Clarion Books, 2000.

Catalanotto, Peter. *Emily's Art.* New York: Atheneum Books, 2001.

Chall, Marsha Wilson. *Up North at the Cabin.* New York: Lothrop, Lee & Shepard Books, 1992.

Chen, Chih-Yuan. *Guji Guji.* La Jolla, CA: Kane/Miller Book Publishers, 2003.

Christelow, Eileen. *What Do Authors Do?* New York: Clarion Books, 1995.

Christelow, Eileen. *What Do Illustrators Do?* New York: Clarion Books, 1999.

Cleary, Beverly. *Dear Mr. Henshaw.* New York: Morrow, 1983.

Cooney, Barbara. *Eleanor.* New York: Scholastic Inc., 1996.

Cooney, Barbara. *Miss Rumphius.* New York: Puffin, 1982.

Cooper, Melrose. *Gettin' Through Thursday.* New York: Lee & Low, 1998.

Creech, Sharon. *Fishing in the Air.* New York: Joanna Cotler Books, 2000.

Creech, Sharon. *Love That Dog.* New York: HarperCollins, 2001.

Crews, Donald. *Bigmama's.* New York: Greenwillow Books, 1991.

Crews, Donald. *The Shortcut.* New York: Greenwillow Books, 1992.

Cronin, Doreen. *Click Clack Moo: Cows That Type.* New York: Simon & Schuster Books for Young Readers, 2000.

Cronin, Doreen. *Diary of a Spider.* New York: Joanna Cotler Books, 2005.

Cronin, Doreen. *Diary of a Worm.* New York: Joanna Cotler Books, 2003.

Crum, Shutta. *The Bravest of the Brave.* New York: Alfred A. Knopf, 2005.

Curtis, Gavin. *The Bat Boy and His Violin*. New York: Aladdin Paperbacks, 1998.

Danneberg, Julie. *First Day Jitters*. Watertown, MA: A Whispering Coyote Book, 2000.

Davies, Nicola. *One Tiny Turtle*. New York: Scholastic Inc., 2001.

Davis, Katie. *Who Hops?* New York: Scholastic Inc., 1998.

Day, Alexandra. *Darby: The Special Order Pup*. New York: Dial Books for Young Readers, 2000.

DeGross, Mona Lisa. *Donovan's Word Jar*. New York: Scholastic Inc., 1994.

dePaola, Tomie. *The Baby Sister*. New York: G. P. Putnam's Sons, 1996.

dePaola, Tomie. *The Quilt Story*. New York: Scholastic Inc., 1996.

Dodd, Anne Wescott. *The Story of the Sea Glass*. Camden, ME: Down East Books, 1999.

Edwards, Pamela Duncan. *Honk!* New York: Hyperion Books, 1998.

Ehrlick, Amy (ed.) *When I Was Your Age (Vol. 1)*. Cambridge, MA: Candlewick Press, 2001.

Ehrlick, Amy (ed.) *When I Was Your Age (Vol. 2)*. Cambridge, MA: Candlewick Press, 2002.

Fitch, Sheree. *No Two Snowflakes*. Victoria, BC, Canada: Orca Book Publishers, 2001.

Fitzpatrick, Marie-Louise. *Lizzy and Skunk*. New York: Dorling Kindersley, 2000.

Fox, Mem. *Harriet, You'll Drive Me Wild*. San Diego: Harcourt Brace, 2000.

Fox, Mem. *Koala Lou*. San Diego: Harcourt Brace Jovanovich, 1989.

Fox, Mem. *Wilfrid Gordon MacDonald Partridge*. Brooklyn: Kane/Miller Book Publishers, 1985.

Frasier, Debra. *Out of the Ocean*. San Diego: Harcourt: 1998.

Fraustino, Lisa Rowe. *The Hickory Chair*. New York: Scholastic Inc., 2001.

Frazee, Marla. *Roller Coaster*. San Diego: Harcourt, 2003.

French, Judy. *Diary of a Wombat*. New York: Clarion Books, 2003.

Friedman, Ina R. *How My Parents Learned to Eat*. Boston: Houghton Mifflin, 1984.

Gray, Libba Moore. *Dear Willie Rudd*. New York: Aladdin Paperbacks, 1993.

Gray, Libba Moore. *My Mama Had a Dancing Heart*. New York: Orchard Books, 1995.

Green, Donna. *The Little Artist*. Mansfield, MA: Fremont & Green Limited, 1999.

Grooms, Molly. *We Are Bears*. Chanhassen, MN: NorthWord Press, 2002.

Haseley, Dennis. *A Story for Bear*. San Diego: Harcourt, Inc., 2002.

Heide, Florence Parry & Gilliland, Judith Heide. *The Day of Ahmed's Secret*. New York: Lothrop, Lee & Shepard, 1990.

Henkes, Kevin. *Grandpa and Bo*. New York: Greenwillow Books, 2002.

Henkes, Kevin. *Kitten's First Full Moon*. New York: Greenwillow Books, 2004.

Henkes, Kevin. *Lilly's Purple Plastic Purse*. New York: Greenwillow Books, 1996.

Hesse, Karen. *The Cats in Krasinski Square*. New York: Scholastic Inc., 2004.

Hesse, Karen. *Letters From Rifka*. New York: Puffin, 1992.

Hesse, Karen. *Out of the Dust*. New York: Scholastic Inc., 1997.

Hest, Amy. *When Jessie Came Across the Sea*. Cambridge, MA: Candlewick, 1997.

Hoose, Phillip & Hannah. *Hey, Little Ant.* Berkeley: Tricycle Press, 1998.

Hopkinson, Deborah. *Fannie in the Kitchen.* New York: Atheneum Books for Young Readers, 1999.

Horowitz, Ruth. *Crab Moon.* Cambridge, MA: Candlewick Press, 2000.

Houston, Gail. *My Great Aunt Arizona.* New York: HarperCollins Publishers, 1992.

Howard, Arthur. *When I Was Five.* San Diego: Harcourt Brace, 1996.

Hundal, Nancy. *Camping.* Ontario, Canada: Fitzhenry & Whiteside, 2001.

Hunter, Shaun. *Writers.* New York: Crabtree Publishing Company, 1998.

Hutchins, Hazel. *One Dark Night.* New York: Viking, 2001.

Inkpen, Deborah. *Harriet.* Hauppauge, New York: Barron's, 1998.

James, Simon. *Dear Mr. Blueberry.* New York: McElderry Books, 1991.

Johnston, Angela. *The Leaving Morning.* New York: Orchard Books, 1992.

Johnston, Angela. *Tell Me a Story, Mama.* New York: Orchard Books, 1988.

Johnson, Paul Brett & Lewis, Celeste. *Lost.* New York: Orchard Books, 1996.

Johnston, Tony. *Amber on the Mountain.* New York: Penguin, 1994.

Johnston, Tony. *The Barn Owls.* Watertown, MA: Charlesbridge, 2000.

Joosse, Barbara. *I Love You the Purplest.* San Francisco: Chronicle Books, 1996.

Kalman, Maira. *Fireboat.* New York: Scholastic Inc., 2002.

Krosoczka, Jarrett J. *Baghead.* New York: Alfred A. Knopf, 2002.

Krull, Kathleen. *Wilma Unlimited.* San Diego: Harcourt Brace, 1996.

LaMarche, Jim. *The Raft.* New York: HarperCollins, 2000.

Laminack, Lester. *The Sunsets of Miss Olivia Wiggins.* Atlanta: Peachtree, 1998.

Larios, Julie. *Have You Ever Done That?* Asheville, NC: Front Street, 2001.

L'Engle, Madeleine. *The Other Dog.* New York: Sea Star Books, 2001.

Lester, Alison. *Imagine.* Boston: Houghton Mifflin, 1989.

Lester, Helen. *Author: A True Story.* Boston: Houghton Mifflin, 1997.

Levinson, Riki. *Watch the Stars Come Out.* New York: Dutton, 1985.

Little, Jean. *Hey World, Here I Am.* New York: The Trumpet Club, 1986.

Locker, Thomas. *Mountain Dance.* San Diego: Silver Whistle/Harcourt, 2001.

London, Jonathan. *Puddles.* New York: Puffin Books, 1997.

London, Jonathan. *Tell Me a Story.* Katonah: NY: Richard C. Owens, 1998.

Loufane. *Lola.* Wheaton, IL: Me + Mi Publishing, Inc., 2006.

Lowry, Lois. *Number the Stars.* Boston: Houghton Mifflin, 1989.

MacLachlan, Patricia. *All the Places to Love.* New York: HarperCollins, 1994.

MacLachlan, Patricia. *Once I Ate a Pie.* New York: Harper Collins, 2006.

MacLachlan, Patricia. *Painting the Wind.* New York: J. Cotler Books, 2003.

MacLachlan, Patricia. *The Sick Day.* New York: Random House Children's Books, 2001.

MacLachlan, Patricia. *What You Know First.* New York: Harper Collins, 1995.

Manson, Ainslie & Dean Griffiths. *Ballerinas Don't Wear Glasses*. Victoria, BC: Orca Book Publishers, 2000.

Marcus, Leonard S. *Author Talk*. New York: Simon & Schuster Books for Young Readers, 2000.

Marcus, Leonard S. *The Making of Goodnight Moon*. New York: HarperTrophy, 1997.

Martin, Bill Jr. *Brown Bear, Brown Bear, What Do You See?* New York: Henry Holt & Co., 1992.

Martin, Bill Jr. *Chicka Chicka Boom Boom*. New York: Simon & Schuster, 1989.

Martin, Bill Jr. *Knots on a Counting Rope*. New York: Henry Holt, 1987.

Martin, Jacqueline Briggs. *On Sand Island*. Boston: Houghton Mifflin, 2003.

Mathis, Sharon Bell. *Sidewalk Story*. New York: Puffin Books, 1986.

McCloskey, Robert. *Make Way for Ducklings*. New York: Viking Press, 1969.

McKissack, Patricia. *Can You Imagine?* Katonah, NY: Richard C. Owens, 1997.

McSwigan, Marie. *Snow Treasure*. New York: Scholastic, 1942.

Miller, Margaret. *Now I'm Big*. New York: Greenwillow Books, 1996.

Moss, Marissa. *Amelia's Notebook*. Berkeley, CA: Tricycle Press, 1995.

Munsch, Robert. *Mmm, Cookies*. New York: Scholastic Inc., 2000.

Naylor, Phyllis Reynolds. *How I Came to Be a Writer*. New York: Scholastic Inc., 1992.

Nicholls, Judith. *Billywise*. New York: Bloomsbury, 2002.

Nixon, Joan Lowry. *If You Were a Writer*. New York: Simon & Schuster Books for Young Readers, 1988.

Orloff, Karen Kaufman. *I Wanna Iguana*. New York: G. P. Putnam's Sons, 2004.

Pallotta, Jerry. *Dory Story*. Watertown, MA: Charlesbridge, 2000.

Paulsen, Gary. *Canoe Days*. New York: Doubleday, 1999.

Pearson, Susan. *Silver Morning*. San Diego: Harcourt Brace, 1998.

Pilkey, Dav. *Dog Breath*. New York: Blue Sky Press, 1994.

Pilkey, Dav. *The Paperboy*. New York: Orchard Books, 1996.

Pinkney, Andrea Davis. *Duke Ellington*. New York: Hyperion Books for Children, 1998.

Pittman, Helena Clare. *One Quiet Morning*. Minneapolis: Carolrhoda Books, Inc., 1996.

Polacco, Patricia. *Firetalking*. Katonah, NY: Richard C. Owens, 1994.

Polacco, Patricia. *My Rotten Redheaded Older Brother*. New York: Simon & Schuster, 1994.

Polacco, Patricia. *Thunder Cake*. New York: Philomel Books, 1990.

Prap, Lila. *Why?* La Jolla, CA: Kane/Miller Book Publishers, Inc., 2005.

Pulver, Robin & Reed, Lynn Rowe. *Punctuation Takes a Vacation*. New York: Holiday House, 2003.

Ray, Mary Lyn. *Red Rubber Boot Day*. Orlando: Voyager Books, 2000.

Reading Is Fundamental. *The Art of Reading*. New York: Dutton Books, 2005.

Rey, Margret & Shalleck, Alan J. *Curious George at the Ballet*. Boston: Houghton Mifflin, 1986.

Reynolds, Peter H. *ish*. Cambridge, MA: Candlewick Press, 2004.

Ringgold, Faith. *Tar Beach*. New York: Crown Publishers, 1991.

Ryan, Pam Muñoz. *Hello Ocean*. Watertown, MA: Charlesbridge Publishing, 2001.

Ryan, Pamela. *Chasing the Alphabet: The Story of Children's Author Jerry Pallotta*. Boston, MA: Shining Sea Press, 1993.

Ryder, Joanne. *Little Panda*. New York: Simon & Schuster, 2001.

Ryder, Joanne. *My Father's Hands*. New York: Morrow Jr. Books, 1994.

Rylant, Cynthia. *Best Wishes*. Katonah, NY: Richard C. Owens, 1992.

Rylant, Cynthia. *Birthday Presents*. New York: Orchard Books, 1987.

Rylant, Cynthia. *The Great Gracie Chase*. New York: Blue Sky Press, 2001.

Rylant, Cynthia. *Henry and Mudge: The First Book*. New York: Simon & Schuster, 1987.

Rylant, Cynthia. *In November*. San Diego: Harcourt Brace, 2000.

Rylant, Cynthia. *Long Night Moon*. New York: Simon & Schuster Books for Young Readers, 2004.

Rylant, Cynthia. *Night in the Country*. New York: Bradbury Press, 1986.

Rylant, Cynthia. *The Relatives Came*. New York: Macmillan, 1985.

Rylant, Cynthia. *Scarecrow*. San Diego: Harcourt Brace, 1998.

Rylant, Cynthia. *Silver Packages*. New York: Orchard Books, 1997.

Rylant, Cynthia. *Tulip Sees America*. New York: Blue Sky Press, 1998.

Rylant, Cynthia. *The Whales*. New York: Blue Sky Press, 1996.

Rylant, Cynthia. *When I Was Young in the Mountains*. New York: Aladdin Books, 1991.

Sams, Carl. *Lost in the Woods*. Milford, MI: C. R. Sams II Photography, 2004

Sams, Carl. *Stranger in the Woods*. Milford, MI: C. R. Sams II Photography, 2000.

Say, Allen. *Grandfather's Journey*. Boston: Houghton Mifflin, 1993.

Sayre, April Pulley. *Turtle, Turtle, Watch Out!* New York: Orchard Books, 2000.

Schotter, Roni. *Nothing Ever Happens on 90th Street*. New York: Orchard Books, 1997.

Seuling, Barbara. *Winter Lullaby*. San Diego: Browndeer Press, 1998.

Shannon, David. *David Goes to School*. New York: Blue Sky Press, 1999.

Simon, Seymour. *From Paper Airplanes to Outer Space*. Richard C. Owens, 2000.

Simont, Marc. *The Stray Dog*. New York: HarperCollins, 2001.

Stevens, Janet. *My Big Dog*. New York: My Golden Book, 1999.

Stevens, Janet. *From Pictures to Words*. New York: Holiday House, 1995.

Stewart, Sarah. *The Gardener*. New York: Farrar, Straus & Giroux, 1995.

Stewart, Sarah. *The Journey*. New York: Farrar, Straus & Giroux, 2001.

Stilton, Geronimo. *Lost Treasure of the Emerald Eye*. New York: Scholastic Inc., 2000.

Stojic, Manya. *Rain*. New York: Crown Publishers, Inc., 2000.

Stolz, Mary. *Storm in the Night*. New York: HarperCollins, 1988.

Thomas, Jane Resh. *The Comeback Dog*. New York: Houghton Mifflin/Clarion Books, 1981.

Truss, Lynne & Timmons, Bonnie. *Eats, Shoots & Leaves: Why, Commas Really Do Make a Difference!* New York: G. P. Putnam's Sons, 2006

Viorst, Judith. *Alexander and the Terrible, Horrible, No Good, Very Bad Day*. New York: Atheneum Books, 1972.

Viorst, Judith. *Earrings!* New York: Atheneum Books, 1990.

Ward, Cindy. *Cookie's Week*. New York: Scholastic Inc., 1990

Whatley, Bruce. *Little White Dogs Can't Jump*. Australia: HarperCollins, 2001.

Wheeler, Lisa. *Porcupining*. Boston: Little, Brown & Company, 2002.

White, E. B. *Charlotte's Web*. New York: Harper & Row, 1952.

Wiesmuller, Dieter. *In the Blink of an Eye*. New York: Walker and Company, 2002.

Willems, Mo. *Knuffle Bunny*. New York: Scholastic Inc., 2004.

Williams, Vera. *A Chair for My Mother*. New York: Greenwillow Books, 1982.

Williams, Vera. *Stringbean's Trip to the Shining Sea*. New York: Greenwillow Books, 1988.

Williams, Vera. *Three Days on a River in a Red Canoe*. New York: Greenwillow Books, 1981.

Wong, Janet S. *The Trip Back Home*. San Diego: Harcourt, 2000.

Wood, Douglas. *A Quiet Place*. New York: Simon & Schuster, 2002.

Woodruff, Elvira. *Dear Levi*. New York: Knopf, 1994.

Wright-Frierson, Virginia. *The Desert Scrapbook*. New York: Simon & Schuster Books for Young Readers, 1996.

Wright-Frierson, Virginia. *The Island Scrapbook*. New York: Simon & Schuster Books for Young Readers, 1998.

Yolen, Jane. *A Letter From Phoenix Farm*. Katonah, NY: Richard C. Owens,1992.

Yolen, Jane. *Letting Swift River Go*. Boston: Little, Brown, 1991.

Yolen, Jane. *Miz Berlin Walks*. New York: Philomel Books, 1997

Yolen, Jane. *Owl Moon*. New York: Philomel Books, 1987.

Yolen, Jane. *Welcome to the Green House*. New York: Paper Star Books, 1993.

Young, Carol. *Little Walrus Warning*. New York: Scholastic Inc., 1996.

Young, Ed. *Seven Blind Mice*. New York: Philomel Books, 1991.